ARTIFICIAL INTELLIGENCE

COLLECTION

HISTORICAL DATA IN DATABASES FOR AI

STRUCTURES, PRESERVATION AND PURGE

Prof. Marcão - Marcus Vinícius Pinto

Disclaimer.

Please note that the information contained in this document is for educational and entertainment purposes only. Every effort has been made to provide complete, accurate, up-to-date, and reliable information. No warranty of any kind is express or implied.

By reading this text, the reader agrees that under no circumstances is the author liable for any losses, direct or indirect, incurred as a result of the use of the information contained in this book, including, but not limited to, errors, omissions, or inaccuracies.

ISBN: 9798340675491

Publishing imprint: Independently published

Summary

Welcome.

We live in an unprecedented era, where the amount of information generated every second exceeds by many orders of magnitude everything that has been accumulated over the millennia of human civilization.

We are immersed in an ocean of data, which grows at an overwhelming rate and extends across all facets of modern life. This dizzying growth, driven by digitalization, the Internet of Things (IoT), social networks, and Artificial Intelligence (AI), presents us with a monumental challenge: how to preserve this vast legacy of information for future generations?

This book, "Historical Data in Databases for AI: Structures, Preservation, and Purge," is a critical reflection on this new landscape. By diving into how personalization algorithms work and the implications they bring to our digital freedom, we aim to offer more than a diagnosis of the impact of these technologies.

If data is the new oil, as many like to claim, then historical data is the cultural and intellectual heritage of humanity, which we must protect with the same zeal with which we preserve our works of art, our monuments, and our literature.

Historical data is much more than simple records of the past; They are the foundation on which we build new ideas, formulate hypotheses, and make decisions that affect the course of our lives and the societies in which we live.

They provide the context needed to understand the present and predict the future. Without a clear and detailed understanding of what happened before, we are at the mercy of the unknown, unable to learn from the mistakes and successes of the past.

In fields such as healthcare, historical data allows for the analysis of disease patterns and the effectiveness of treatments over time, enabling significant advances in medicine.

In economics, they are essential for predicting market trends, assessing risks, and making informed decisions that influence public policy and business strategies. In science, they are the basis for developing theories and validating hypotheses that can change our understanding of the universe.

However, the preservation of this data is not a simple task. It requires a combination of advanced technologies, effective management strategies, and a deep respect for the ethical and legal implications involved in handling sensitive information. This book offers a detailed guide to navigating these challenges, providing insights and best practices that can be applied across a variety of industries.

The journey to preserve historical data begins with recognizing its intrinsic value. It is not enough to simply store data; It is necessary to ensure that they are preserved with integrity, safely accessible and usable for future generations.

This involves the implementation of cutting-edge technologies such as cloud storage, blockchain, and even the emerging DNA storage, which promise to transform the way we preserve large volumes of data over time.

But technology alone is not enough. The preservation of historical data is, above all, an act of responsibility. As stewards of this data, we have an obligation to ensure that it is protected from obsolescence, corruption and loss.

This means implementing robust data governance policies, compliance with international regulations, and expungement strategies that respect both the privacy of individuals and the need to maintain valuable information.

This book explores all of these facets of historical data preservation, offering a comprehensive overview of the best practices and technologies available, while also addressing the ethical and social complexities that permeate this task.

The preservation of historical data, when done correctly, is not only a legal obligation, but a service to society. It allows future generations to access accumulated knowledge, learn from it, and continue to expand the frontiers of human knowledge. Thus, this book is also a call for all professionals involved in this area to adopt an approach that combines technical excellence with a deep ethical awareness.

Whether you're an IT manager, an archivist, a data scientist, a researcher, or a student, we hope this book serves as a guide and a source of inspiration. May you use the knowledge shared here to not only preserve the past, but also to shape a future in which access to knowledge is universal, safe, and seamless.

The road ahead is fraught with challenges, but also with opportunities. By embarking on this journey of preserving historical data, you become a custodian of our collective legacy and an architect of the future. May this responsibility inspire you to innovate, protect, and perpetuate the knowledge that defines who we are and what we can achieve.

This book is therefore not just a technical work, but a call to action. A call for us to build a future together in which the past is always a source of wisdom, the present a field of responsible action, and the future a blank canvas ready to be painted with the colors of innovation, knowledge and ethics.

I conclude with a reflection:

Artificial intelligence is not just a field of study or an emerging technology; It is a new paradigm that is reshaping the way we interact with the world and with each other.

Understanding its fundamentals – from the most basic data to the most complex algorithms – is not just a professional skill, but a necessity for any citizen of the twenty-first century.

However, this is just one step in an essential journey in the field of artificial intelligence. This volume is part of a larger collection, "Artificial Intelligence: The Power of Data," with 49 volumes that explore, in depth, different aspects of AI and data science.

The other volumes address equally crucial topics, such as the integration of AI systems, predictive analytics, and the use of advanced algorithms for decision-making.

By purchasing and reading the other books in the collection, you will have a holistic and deep view that will allow you not only to optimize data governance, but also to enhance the impact of artificial intelligence on your operations.

I wish you a good reading, a good learning and good projects.

Prof. Marcão - Marcus Vinícius Pinto

M.Sc. in Information Technology
Specialist in Information Technology.
Consultant, Mentor and Speaker on Artificial Intelligence,
Information Architecture and Data Governance.
Founder, CEO, teacher and
pedagogical advisor at MVP Consult.

1 The hidden power of the past: the centrality of historical data in Artificial Intelligence.

At the heart of contemporary technological evolution, historical data emerges as crucial elements in the construction and refinement of Artificial Intelligence (AI) systems.

Data, which encapsulates the wealth of information accumulated over time, allows information systems and now artificial intelligence to transcend the present, integrating past knowledge to project and predict possible futures.

The importance of historical data is vast and multifaceted, ranging from the lifeline of transactional databases and the training of machine learning models to the interpretation and contextualization of new data in real time.

Historically, the relevance of historical data in computing was not immediately recognized. During the early decades of computing, data was often treated as temporal entities, stored only for as long as necessary to fulfill their immediate functions.

However, as information systems began to develop and gain complexity, it became apparent that processing power and strategic and managerial reporting depended largely on the ability to access and analyze past patterns.

Historical data is critical, for example, in the financial sector, where predictive models rely on analyzing market data accumulated over decades to predict economic trends and detect emerging risks.

Nowadays, an AI model used by a financial institution can, through a thorough analysis of historical data, identify patterns of behavior associated with economic crises, allowing informed decisions to be made proactively.

Similarly, in the field of health, historical data have played a transformative role. The ability to analyze medical records spanning decades makes it possible for AI systems to identify risk factors, predict disease outbreaks, and propose personalized treatments.

The use of historical data in predictive diagnoses is exemplified by systems such as IBM Watson, which relies on vast amounts of medical data accumulated over time to suggest diagnoses and treatment options for patients.

Another notable example is the use of historical data in public safety systems, where AI can analyze crime records over the years to predict where and when crimes are most likely to occur. This analysis allows security forces to allocate resources more efficiently, preventing incidents before they occur.

Therefore, historical data is not just an additional feature; they are the backbone upon which many advanced AI applications are built.

The absence of a deep understanding of historical data can result in AI models that, while accurate in the short term, fail to capture the depth and complexity of the phenomena they seek to model.

1.1   Evolution of databases and the processing of historical data.

The history of computing is largely the history of the evolution of databases. From the earliest data storage systems, which were simple and limited, to sophisticated modern databases, the ability to manage and process large volumes of historical data has been a crucial factor in the development of AI technologies.

In the early days, databases were designed to meet specific and immediate needs, with little regard for the preservation and use of data over time.

Early database management systems (DBMS), such as the IBM IMS (Information Management System), developed in the 1960s, were well-suited for operational tasks, but lacked the flexibility needed to handle the complexity of historical data.

It was only with the introduction of relational databases in the 1970s and 1980s that systems began to incorporate mechanisms for efficient data storage and retrieval over time.

The relational model, proposed by Edgar F. Codd, represented a revolution by allowing structured data to be stored in a way that facilitated consultation and manipulation, becoming the basis for the development of DBMSs such as Oracle and SQL Server.

These databases allowed data to be stored in a more organized and accessible way, but a robust approach to historical data management was still lacking.

With the advent of Big Data technologies and the growing need to store and process massive volumes of information, new approaches to the treatment of historical data have emerged.

NoSQL databases such as MongoDB and Cassandra have enabled the management of large volumes of unstructured data, offering flexibility and scalability that traditional relational databases could not provide.

However, despite these innovations, the proper treatment of historical data remains a challenge. Maintaining temporal integrity and the ability to perform efficient historical queries are areas that require advanced data management techniques, such as the use of temporal and versioning tables, which allow changes in data over time to be tracked and analyzed.

Additionally, integrating historical data into AI systems requires a careful approach to ensure that models are able to correctly interpret the nuances of past data.

This includes the use of techniques such as data normalization, which adjusts historical data so that it is comparable with current data, and interpolation, which allows you to fill in gaps in incomplete historical data sets.

1.2   Challenges and opportunities in the processing of historical data.

The management of historical data in databases for AI presents a series of technical and conceptual challenges that need to be faced so that these systems can operate effectively. One of the main challenges is the scale of the data.

With the exponential growth in the amount of data generated, the storage and processing of historical data has become increasingly complex. This is especially true in industries such as the Internet of Things (IoT), where sensors and devices generate continuous streams of data that need to be stored and analyzed over time.

Another significant challenge is performance. As historical datasets grow, queries and analysis become slower, impacting the ability of AI systems to provide real-time results.

This requires the implementation of advanced query indexing and optimization techniques, as well as the use of in-memory data storage technologies, which can speed up access to historical data.

Data integrity is also a central concern. Ensuring that historical data is preserved without loss of accuracy or context is crucial to the reliability of AI systems. This involves implementing auditing and version control mechanisms, which allow you to track and verify changes in data over time.

On the other hand, historical data also offers significant opportunities. Longitudinal analysis of historical data can reveal patterns that would not be visible in an analysis limited to current data.

This is particularly important in areas such as scientific research, where the ability to analyze large volumes of historical data can lead to new discoveries and breakthroughs.

In addition, historical data is essential for creating robust predictive models. The ability to learn from the past allows AI systems to make more accurate and informed predictions, better adapting to new data and situations.

This is exemplified by the use of historical data in deep learning models, such as those employed by systems such as ChatGPT, which utilizes vast sets of historical textual data to generate contextually relevant responses.

Systems such as ChatGPT, developed by OpenAI, and Claude AI, developed by Anthropic, illustrate how integrating historical data can enhance AI's ability to generate more accurate and contextual responses.

These systems draw on vast repositories of textual data accumulated over years, using them to learn language and context patterns that are applied to their interactions.

The ability to "remember" and apply historical knowledge in new contexts is what differentiates these models from systems that operate only with contemporary data.

However, the use of historical data also raises ethical and technical issues, such as the management of biases. Historical data can reflect the biases and inequalities of the past, and these biases can be perpetuated or amplified by AI systems if not properly addressed.

Mitigating these biases requires a careful approach in the selection and treatment of historical data, as well as in the construction of AI models.

2 Time architectures: database structures for storing and processing historical data.

"Past: it is the future used."
Millor Fernandes

Relational databases have been, since their inception, the cornerstone of information management in corporate and scientific environments. Introduced by Edgar F. Codd in the 1970s, relational databases are structured around the concept of tables that organize data into rows and columns, allowing for efficient querying and structured manipulation of information.

This model, despite being created to manage operational data, has evolved to support the complexity of historical data, which is fundamental for the development of robust and accurate Artificial Intelligence (AI) systems.

2.1 Temporal tables and versioning: guardians of history.

One of the most significant innovations in relational databases for dealing with historical data is the introduction of temporal tables and versioning mechanisms.

Temporal tables are designed to store not only the current value of a piece of data, but also all of its previous versions, allowing users to query the state of a piece of data at any point in time.

This functionality is crucial for the preservation of temporal integrity, ensuring that AI systems can access and analyze data in its original historical context.

The use of temporal tables is widely discussed in the database literature, with authors such as Richard T. Snodgrass, who developed the concept of "time-oriented databases" and presented methodologies for the effective implementation of such systems.

These tables allow complex queries to be performed, such as reconstructing a view of the database at a specific time in the past, which is vital for audits, trend analysis, and training AI models that require a comprehensive time perspective.

Versioning is another technique that complements temporal storage by allowing multiple versions of a record to be maintained, each representing a significant change over time.

This is particularly useful in version control systems, where data evolution needs to be closely monitored, such as in document management systems, financial applications, and, increasingly, in AI applications that require a detailed understanding of changes in historical data.

Despite the undeniable advantages of relational databases in managing historical data, they also present significant challenges. One of the main problems is performance.

As the volume of historical data grows, query and manipulation operations become slower, requiring constant optimizations.

Temporal indexes and data partitioning are some of the techniques used to mitigate these issues, but the inherent complexity of these solutions can limit their applicability in large-scale scenarios.

Another challenge is the rigidity of the relational model, which, despite its clear and defined structure, may not be flexible enough to deal with the diversity and variability of historical data in certain contexts, such as those found in unstructured or semi-structured environments.

This aspect will be explored in more detail throughout this chapter when we discuss NoSQL databases.

2.2 NoSQL databases and the treatment of historical data in non-relational environments.

The explosion of data in recent decades, driven by the internet, social networks, and mobile devices, has exposed the limitations of traditional relational databases and paved the way for the development of NoSQL databases.

These foundations, which include MongoDB, Cassandra, and HBase, are designed to handle massive volumes of unstructured or semi-structured data, offering flexibility and scalability that relational systems could not provide.

2.2.1 Flexible structure and scalability: advantages of NoSQL systems.

One of the most outstanding features of NoSQL databases is their ability to store and manage large amounts of data without the need for a rigid schema.

This is particularly advantageous when it comes to historical data, which can vary significantly in structure over time.

For example, in a system that stores user activity logs over years, data formats may evolve as new functionality is added, something that would be difficult to accommodate in a traditional relational model.

Horizontal scalability is another significant advantage of NoSQL foundations. Unlike relational databases, which generally scale up (i.e., require more powerful hardware), NoSQL bases can scale out, adding more servers to the database cluster.

This allows large volumes of historical data to be distributed and managed efficiently, maintaining performance even as data grows exponentially.

2.2.2   Challenges and limitations: flexibility commitments.

As you would expect, the flexibility and scalability of NoSQL systems come with some compromises. One of the main challenges is the lack of strong consistency, which is often sacrificed for the sake of availability and fault tolerance.

In systems where the temporal accuracy and consistency of historical data are critical, such as in financial or legal applications, this limitation may be unacceptable.

In addition, the absence of a rigid schema can lead to additional complexity in data management and querying.

Lack of normalization, which is a common practice in relational databases, can result in data redundancy and ultimately greater difficulty maintaining the integrity of historical data over time.

Data warehouses, on the other hand, have been a popular solution for storing and analyzing large volumes of data, especially in contexts where it is necessary to integrate and consolidate data from multiple sources for complex analysis.

These platforms are designed to store large volumes of historical data, organized in a way that supports sophisticated analytical queries.

The primary strength of data warehouses lies in their ability to integrate data from multiple sources, providing a comprehensive and consolidated view of operations and performance over time.

This is crucial in industries such as retail, where analyzing sales trends over years can reveal seasonal and behavioral patterns that influence business decisions.

Data Warehouses use schemas such as star schema and snowflake schema to organize data, making it easier to run complex queries. They also allow the creation of OLAP (Online Analytical Processing) cubes, which provide multidimensional views of historical data, allowing analysts to explore information from different temporal perspectives.

Despite their robustness, data warehouses face significant challenges when it comes to scalability and maintaining performance with the increasing volume of historical data.

The workload associated with ETLs (Extract, Transform, Load), which are the processes of collecting, transforming, and loading data into the warehouse, can become a bottleneck as the volume of data increases.

Solutions such as the use of Data Lakes in conjunction with Data Warehouses, where the data lake acts as a repository for large volumes of raw data, have been implemented to mitigate these challenges.

Another challenge is maintaining data integrity over time. As historical data accumulates, the possibility of data corruption or inconsistencies increases.

This requires the implementation of strict quality control and auditing policies, as well as redundant storage technologies to ensure that historical data remains healthy and accessible.

2.3   Real-time databases and synchronization with historical data.

The need to make real-time decisions has led to the development of real-time databases, which are designed to provide near-instantaneous responses to queries and data operations.

However, integrating historical data with real-time data presents unique challenges, especially in terms of consistency and temporal coherence.

2.3.1   Temporal synchronization: uniting the past and the present.

Synchronizing historical data with real-time data requires implementing strategies that ensure that information is consistent over time.

One common approach is the use of data pipelines that feed both real-time systems and historical data repositories. These pipelines process and transform the data in real-time before storing it in a format that can be integrated with historical data.

In the context of AI, this synchronization is critical for creating models that can make accurate predictions based on up-to-date data.

For example, in a demand forecasting system, historical data is used to train the model, while real-time data allows the model to make instant adjustments for changes in market conditions.

2.3.2   Challenges and solutions: Maintaining consistency and performance.

One of the biggest challenges in synchronizing historical data with real-time data is maintaining consistency between the two. Conflicts can arise if real-time data is not properly integrated into histories, leading to inconsistencies that can compromise the integrity of the AI system.

To overcome these challenges, techniques such as "eventual consistency" and the use of distributed transaction logs are often employed.

"Eventual consistency" allows systems to be more tolerant of synchronization failures and delays, while transaction logs ensure that all changes are recorded and can be reconciled later, maintaining data coherence over time.

2.4   Choosing the right architecture.

The choice of database architecture for the storage and processing of historical data is a critical decision that should be based on the specific needs of the AI application, as well as the characteristics of the data that will be managed.

Relational databases offer structure and precision, but they can be limited in terms of scalability and flexibility. NoSQL systems provide flexibility and scalability, but can sacrifice consistency and temporal integrity.

Data warehouses offer a robust solution for integrated analytics, but face scalability challenges and management complexity. Finally, real-time databases allow for immediate decisions, but require careful synchronization with historical data to maintain consistency.

A deep understanding of these architectures and their impacts on the treatment of historical data is essential for the success of AI systems, especially in a world where the amount of data grows exponentially and the need for historical analysis becomes increasingly relevant.

3 Saving time: processing and preserving the data timeline.

The concept of time, although abstract in its nature, plays a key role in the processing of historical data. In the context of artificial intelligence (AI), the ability to capture, preserve, and analyze data over time is essential to ensure the accuracy and relevance of algorithmic decisions.

Temporal data modeling emerges as a critical approach to deal with the complexity of temporality in AI systems, allowing time to become an explicit dimension in the storage and consultation of data.

3.1 Temporal modeling techniques: timestamps and time intervals.

One of the most basic and widely used techniques in temporal modeling is assigning timestamps to data. A timestamp is essentially a timestamp that indicates the exact moment when a piece of data was created, modified, or observed. This technique is particularly useful in systems that require a detailed history of events, such as user activity logs or financial records.

More advanced techniques involve the use of time intervals, which are periods during which a particular piece of data is considered valid. For example, a contract may have a start date and an end date, and any query to that contract should consider those dates to determine its validity at the time of the query.

The use of time intervals is common in temporal databases, which are designed to manage and query data that varies over time.

Richard T. Snodgrass, one of the pioneers in the field of temporal databases, proposed the incorporation of two main temporal dimensions: valid time, which refers to the period in which a fact is true in the real world, and transaction time, which indicates the moment when the fact was stored in the database.

Integrating these dimensions into a data model allows for the creation of systems that can accurately capture the evolution of data over time.

3.2   Temporal Modeling Patterns.

In addition to specific techniques, temporal modeling standards such as version history and auditing are essential to ensure the integrity and transparency of data over time.

Version history allows multiple versions of a piece of data to be kept, each reflecting the state of the data at a given point in time. This approach is essential for applications where it is necessary to track changes over time, such as in version control systems or in legal document repositories.

Auditing, on the other hand, involves creating detailed records that document all the changes made to a dataset over time.

These records are used for auditing and compliance purposes, ensuring that all changes are traceable and verifiable.

In the context of AI, auditing is particularly important to ensure that models are utilizing accurate and reliable data, especially in regulated industries such as finance and healthcare.

3.3   Consistency and temporal integrity in databases.

Data consistency and integrity are key pillars in building robust and reliable AI systems. When it comes to historical data, these issues become even more complex, as it is necessary to ensure that temporal relationships and dependencies between data are maintained over time.

Preserving temporal coherence requires a rigorous approach that combines modeling techniques with data storage and retrieval strategies.

Data synchronization is an essential technique to ensure that all systems that use historical data are operating with up-to-date and consistent information.

In distributed systems, where data can be stored in different geographic locations, temporal synchronization ensures that all replicas of the data conform to the current state of historical data. This is particularly important in AI systems that rely on real-time and historical data to make decisions.

Version control, as mentioned earlier, also plays a crucial role in maintaining temporal consistency.

By allowing different versions of a piece of data to coexist, systems can track how information has evolved over time and ensure that queries to historical data return results that accurately reflect the state of the data at the time of interest.

3.4   Temporal integrity: auditing and validating data.

Temporal integrity of data refers to the accuracy and reliability of information over time. To maintain temporal integrity, AI systems must implement robust data auditing and validation mechanisms.

Auditing involves the detailed recording of all operations performed on a dataset, allowing any changes to be tracked and verified. This is a key aspect of ensuring regulatory compliance and transparency of AI systems.

Data validation is another essential technique to ensure temporal integrity. This involves continuously verifying that the data stored in the system is correct and complete, and that it accurately reflects the events and transactions that have occurred over time.

In AI systems, data validation is crucial to prevent decisions from being made based on incorrect or incomplete information, which could lead to catastrophic errors.

3.5   Timeline preservation in distributed systems.

Timeline preservation in distributed systems is a significant challenge, due to the complexity of coordinating and synchronizing data across different geographic locations and system components.

However, maintaining a consistent timeline is essential to ensure that AI systems can operate effectively and reliably, regardless of the location of the data.

In distributed systems, data synchronization is critical to ensuring that all replicas of the data are up-to-date and consistent. This is particularly important when it comes to historical data, where accuracy and temporal coherence are essential for analysis and decision-making.

Data synchronization in distributed environments can be achieved through a variety of techniques, including data replication and the use of distributed transaction logs.

Data replication involves creating copies of the data in multiple locations, ensuring that the data is available and accessible, even in the event of system failures.

However, data replication also presents challenges, such as the need to ensure that all copies of the data are synchronized and up-to-date.

Distributed transaction logs are another essential technique for data synchronization in distributed systems. These logs record all transactions performed on a dataset and allow changes to be propagated to all replicas of the data. This ensures that all copies of the data are consistent and that operations can be rolled back in case of errors or failures.

Ensuring temporal consistency across distributed systems is a complex challenge, due to the need to coordinate operations across different locations and ensure that all replicas of the data are compliant with the timeline.

Eventual consistency is a common approach to solving this problem, allowing systems to eventually become consistent even if there are delays in the propagation of changes.

However, eventual consistency may not be sufficient for all AI systems, especially those that require rigorous temporal accuracy.

In such cases, it is necessary to implement more advanced techniques, such as clock synchronization and the use of distributed consensus algorithms, which ensure that all nodes in the system agree on the current state of the data and the timeline.

3.5.1   Impacts of temporal preservation on the performance of AI systems.

Preserving the timeline of data, while essential to the integrity and reliability of AI systems, can have significant impacts on system performance.

The need to maintain and process large volumes of historical data can lead to performance issues such as slower response times and higher resource consumption.

As historical data volumes grow, AI systems face significant challenges in terms of performance and scalability.

Maintaining an accurate timeline requires storing large amounts of data, which can put a strain on system resources and affect query response time.

To mitigate these issues, AI systems must implement advanced performance optimization techniques, such as temporal indexing and data partitioning.

Temporal indexing involves the creation of indexes that allow for rapid retrieval of data based on its temporal dimension, reducing the time it takes to perform historical queries. Data partitioning, in turn, allows large volumes of data to be broken down into smaller, more manageable chunks, improving system scalability.

3.5.2   Trade-offs between performance and time accuracy.

Preserving the timeline often requires a balance between performance and accuracy. While some applications can tolerate a slight loss of temporal accuracy in exchange for better performance, others, such as financial or medical systems, require rigorous temporal accuracy, regardless of the impact on performance.

This trade-off must be carefully considered when designing AI systems that handle historical data. It is important to assess the specific needs of the application and determine the level of temporal accuracy required, implementing the appropriate optimization techniques to ensure that the system can meet these requirements without compromising performance.

3.6   The timeline as a pillar of artificial intelligence.

Preserving the timeline of data is not just a technical issue, but a fundamental principle that underpins the integrity and effectiveness of AI systems.

As historical data becomes increasingly central to the operation of these systems, the ability to accurately capture, model, and maintain the temporal dimension of data becomes essential.

This chapter explored the various techniques and strategies to ensure temporal coherence, from data modeling to preservation in distributed systems.

Also discussed were the impacts of temporal preservation on the performance of AI systems and the trade-offs needed to balance accuracy and efficiency.

In the end, the timeline is not just a representation of the past; it is the foundation on which future decisions are built. By understanding and applying the techniques discussed in this chapter, AI developers and engineers can create systems that are not only responsive to the present but are also deeply informed by the past, thus ensuring that more robust, reliable, and ethical models are created.

4 Data versioning: safeguarding informational lineage in the age of AI.

In the contemporary scenario, in which artificial intelligence (AI) assumes a central role in decision-making, control over the data that feeds such systems has become not only a technical issue, but also an ethical and strategic one.

Data versioning, largely neglected in public discussions, emerges as a crucial practice for the preservation of data lineage and, consequently, for the integrity of decisions arising from AI systems.

4.1 The ephemeral nature of data and the need for versioning.

Throughout history, humanity has always grappled with the need to record, preserve, and reinterpret information, from ancient manuscripts to vast contemporary digital libraries.

However, with the advent of digital technologies and the exponential growth in the amount of data generated, a new challenge arises: the control and maintenance of the "lineage" of this data.

That is, how do you ensure that previous versions of a dataset, which may have been modified over time, are preserved and accessible for re-evaluation or auditing?

In the context of AI, data traceability is essential. AI models are trained, adjusted, and refined based on large volumes of data, which in turn can undergo various transformations.

These changes may include corrections, enrichment, or deletion of information that, if not properly versioned, compromises the ability to interpret future decisions.

Data versioning, therefore, acts as a key measure to preserve informational lineage, allowing each state of a dataset to be stored and retrieved as needed.

4.2   Versioning and lineage of data in AI.

Data lineage refers to the origin and history of all the transformations that a piece of data goes through, from its collection to its use. This concept is particularly important when it comes to ensuring the reliability and auditability of AI models.

If a model is trained in data that undergoes continuous modifications, how can we ensure the integrity of the decisions made by that model without a detailed record of the changes to each piece of data used in the training process?

Let's imagine a practical scenario in healthcare. Suppose an AI system is trained to aid in the early detection of heart disease by utilizing historical patient data. Over time, new tests are incorporated and old records are corrected.

Without proper versioning of the data, a critical error in the initial collection phase could compromise the accuracy of future diagnoses, and it would be impossible to track which dataset was responsible for a given mistaken decision.

In this context, versioning emerges as an indispensable practice. Every change in the data must be recorded, with all the metadata needed to reconstruct the state of the data at any point in its history.

This process not only ensures the integrity and transparency of the information, but also allows for a historical analysis of mistakes and successes, enabling the continuous improvement of AI models.

4.3   Versioning tools and technologies.

Currently, several technologies have been developed to handle data versioning in an efficient and secure way. Tools like Git, very popular in software development, have inspired solutions for versioning large volumes of data.

However, the challenge in data versioning in AI goes beyond simply storing different versions. There is a pressing need for mechanisms that ensure complete traceability of data transformation and its implications for AI models.

Among the most advanced solutions, tools such as DVC (Data Version Control) stand out, a Git extension for data versioning in machine learning projects, which efficiently integrates version control of both data and AI models.

DVC allows different versions of the data to be retrieved to train or retrain models, ensuring the replicability and auditability of the experiments.

In addition, the concept of "data lineage" has become a central aspect in data governance frameworks.

Solutions such as Apache Atlas and Microsoft Purview were developed with the purpose of tracking the lifecycle of data within an organization, documenting each modification and ensuring that any data can be recovered in its original state if necessary.

4.4   Practical examples of data versioning.

To illustrate the practical impact of data versioning, let's return to the field of health. In drug development, for example, clinical data collected from early trials may undergo a series of revisions and corrections.

Proper versioning of this data is crucial to ensure that future efficacy and safety analyses are conducted based on accurate information. If a clinical trial is reviewed and old data is not properly stored, any error in the first trials can negatively influence the analysis of later results, putting public health at risk.

Another example can be found in the financial sector, where AI models are used to predict market trends and perform automated trades.

If historical transaction data is altered or corrected without proper versioning, decisions based on such data can result in significant financial losses. Internal and external audits rely on the traceability of this data, and the absence of versioning would compromise regulatory compliance.

4.5   Versioning as a guarantee of transparency and reliability.

In addition to its technical importance, data versioning is also a matter of transparency. AI models that make autonomous decisions—whether in healthcare, finance, or any other industry—need to operate with a high level of confidence.

Part of that confidence lies in the ability to reconstruct the exact conditions under which a decision was made. Without adequate versioning, this reconstitution becomes unfeasible, leading to uncertainties and distrust as to the validity of the decisions.

Trust in AI systems is ultimately a reflection of trust in the data that feeds them. By ensuring that all versions of the data are preserved and auditable, we are, in fact, protecting the future of AI.

Versioning offers a safeguard against unintentional errors and malicious manipulations, making it an indispensable element for preserving the integrity of artificial intelligence systems.

5 Data Governance: Pillar of Accountability in the Age of Digital Change.

At the heart of the digital age, data governance emerges as a critical building block for ensuring reliability, integrity, and, above all, accountability for data changes.

If, on the one hand, the exponential growth in the amount of information available offers unprecedented opportunities for more informed decision-making, on the other hand, it brings with it the risk of inadvertent or intentional manipulation of this information, compromising not only the quality of the results obtained, but also the trust in the systems that process them. The Concept of Data Governance.

Data governance refers to the set of policies, processes, and standards that govern the use, quality, security, and integrity of data in an organization.

In a world where data collection and use play a central role in diverse industries — from sectors such as healthcare and finance to AI — it is essential that data is managed responsibly and transparently. Governance, in this context, is not only a technical issue, but also an ethical and legal one.

With the growing reliance on automated and AI systems for complex decision-making, the role of data governance gains even greater relevance.

It is no longer just about ensuring the efficiency of an organization's internal processes, but about ensuring that the data used complies with current ethical and legal standards.

The challenge therefore becomes to ensure that every modification made to a piece of data—whether it's a correction, an update, or a deletion—is adequately documented, so that accountability for those changes can be accurately assigned.

5.1 The Importance of Data Traceability.

In practice, data traceability is one of the main tools of data governance, allowing you to know who, when, and why a change was made.

Traceability is therefore an essential mechanism to ensure the accountability of the agents involved in data management.

A clear example can be found in the healthcare industry, where hospital systems rely on electronic medical records to manage patient care.

The alteration of a clinical data, without proper authorization or justification, can lead to misdiagnoses, inappropriate treatments and, in extreme cases, compromise the patient's life.

Data governance, through its control and traceability policies, allows each modification to be documented, attributing due responsibility to the responsible agent.

This process not only ensures data integrity but also facilitates internal and external audits, promoting transparency and reducing the risk of errors or fraud.

In an environment where data integrity can mean the difference between a correct decision and a catastrophic error, the ability to monitor and track changes is critical.

5.2   Artificial intelligence and data governance.

The application of artificial intelligence further expands the relevance of data governance. In a scenario where AI systems are trained with large volumes of data, any undocumented changes can influence the results generated by these systems.

Data versioning and traceability become even more critical, especially in regulated industries such as finance and healthcare, where compliance with strict regulations is indispensable.

To illustrate, let's imagine an AI model used for credit analysis. This model is trained on historical customer data, such as income, payment history, and consumer behavior.

If the data changes—for example, an update in income figures—without effective governance to track and document that change, the model can produce mistaken predictions, directly affecting lending.

Responsibility for changing the data, in this case, would be difficult to assign without a clear governance policy, which could expose the financial institution to significant legal and financial risks.

The concept of "data lineage" emerges as a vital component within governance. It allows the trajectory of a piece of data to be tracked from the moment of its creation to its last use.

In the case of AI systems, this means the ability to identify which datasets were used in training a model and how that information was manipulated throughout the process.

As a result, data governance offers a level of transparency and control that ensures not only compliance with regulations, but also the efficiency and accuracy of AI systems.

5.3   Data governance policies: good practices.

For data governance to be effective, it is essential that organizations adopt good practices that involve all sectors. The implementation of versioning and data traceability policies, for example, is a fundamental step.

Each change in data should be documented with details about the responsible agent, the reason for the change, and the expected impact. This record allows that, in cases of audits or investigations, it is possible to assign responsibilities with clarity and precision.

Additionally, it is important to establish strict access controls, ensuring that only authorized people can make modifications to the data. This is particularly relevant in environments where data is highly sensitive, such as in the financial sector or healthcare.

Adopting multi-factor authentication and data encryption policies are best practices to ensure that data is not altered or accessed by unauthorized actors.

In terms of governance applied to AI, a practical tip is to implement continuous monitoring of models, documenting not only the data used in training, but also subsequent changes.

Tools such as "Data Version Control" (DVC), which allows the versioning of data in machine learning projects, are excellent allies in maintaining traceability and data governance in AI environments.

With them, you can revert changes, perform detailed audits, and ensure that the model is trained on the correct version of the data.

5.4   Examples of data governance.

Several sectors are already advanced in the implementation of data governance policies. In Europe, with the entry into force of the General Data Protection Regulation (GDPR), organizations across the European Union have been required to review and strengthen their governance policies.

In the banking sector, for example, the traceability of transactions and customer data has become a legal requirement, so as to ensure that any change in records can be audited and justified.

In the United States, the Health Insurance Portability and Accountability Act (HIPAA) imposes strict guidelines on the handling of health data. Hospitals and clinics are required to implement systems that ensure the traceability of medical information, allowing any modification to be monitored and recorded, with a view to ensuring the integrity and confidentiality of the data.

In addition to regulatory compliance, data governance also provides a competitive differentiator. Organizations that adopt transparent and robust governance policies gain the trust of their customers, who feel safer knowing that their data is being handled responsibly.

In the context of AI, this is even more relevant, since the credibility of intelligent systems depends directly on the reliability of the data that feeds them.

5.5   Data governance and ethical accountability.

One cannot talk about data governance without addressing the ethical dimension of accountability for changes in data. In a world where information is constantly manipulated and interpreted by AI algorithms, it is essential for organizations to take responsibility not only for the accuracy of the data, but also for the impacts of its changes.

Indiscriminate use of data can lead to harmful outcomes, such as algorithmic discrimination or unconscious biases that negatively affect vulnerable groups.

Ethical responsibility involves the creation of mechanisms for the continuous review and validation of data, ensuring that any changes are justified and in accordance with ethical principles.

This is especially important in industries such as automated recruitment, where AI-based decisions can impact the lives of individuals directly and significantly.

6 Between memory and oblivion: policies of purge and preservation of historical data.

The concept of data purge refers to the systematic process of eliminating data deemed irrelevant, obsolete, or unnecessary within a database.

This procedure is a critical practice for maintaining Artificial Intelligence (AI) systems and databases in general, ensuring that the data stored is relevant and that the systems remain efficient in terms of performance and operational costs.

The need for data purge arises primarily due to the expansive and cumulative nature of data. As businesses and institutions continue to generate data in exponential amounts, storing irrelevant or outdated information can become a burdensome burden for AI systems, both in terms of storage and processing space.

Outdated data can hinder the performance of systems by reducing the accuracy of predictions, introducing bias, or increasing response times.

For example, in AI systems that rely on large volumes of historical data to provide predictive analytics, the accumulation of obsolete data can interfere with the AI model's ability to identify contemporary patterns.

Entering data that no longer reflects the current reality can cause distortions in the results, leading to suboptimal decisions.

Additionally, data purge is critical to ensuring regulatory compliance and data privacy. Legislation such as the General Data Protection Regulation (GDPR) in the European Union and the General Data Protection Law (LGPD) in Brazil impose strict obligations on data storage, including the deletion of personal information that is no longer necessary for the original purpose of collection.

In this regard, data purge plays a crucial role in responsible data management, protecting privacy, and preventing the misuse of personal information.

6.1   Criteria for the identification of obsolete and irrelevant data.

Identifying which data should be purged requires a careful and well-structured analysis. The criteria for determining whether data is stale or irrelevant vary depending on the context, the nature of the data, and the organization's goals. However, some common factors can be considered:

6.1.1   Time and relevance.

One of the main criteria used to determine data obsolescence is the time factor.

Data that was created or stored a long time ago may no longer reflect today's reality, especially in industries such as finance, marketing, and healthcare, where dynamics are fast and information changes frequently.

For example, a financial transaction that took place five years ago may have little relevance to an AI system that makes predictions about current market behavior.

6.1.2   Legal validity and regulatory compliance.

Another important criterion is the legal validity of the data. In many cases, regulations impose specific time limits for data retention. After this period expires, the data may become legally irrelevant and must be deleted.

Compliance with data protection regulations, such as the GDPR, also requires that personal information be deleted when there is no longer justification for its storage.

6.1.3   Operational utility.

The operational usefulness of the data is also a determining factor. Data that is no longer used for operational processes or for the generation of strategic value may be considered irrelevant.

For example, in customer service AI systems, records of interactions that are no longer relevant to the training of the models can be purged without impairing the functionality of the system.

6.2   Purge techniques in relational and non-relational databases.

Data purge can be implemented in a variety of ways, depending on the database architecture used. Approaches vary between relational and non-relational systems, each with its own challenges and advantages.

6.2.1   Purge in relational databases.

In relational databases, purge is typically performed through SQL queries that identify and remove records based on specific criteria, such as the date of creation or the relevance of the data.

For example, in a financial database, you can use a query to exclude all transactions made before a specific date.

One of the most common techniques in relational databases is physical deletion, where the data is completely removed from the system. However, an alternative to this approach is logical deletion, where data is marked as "deleted" or "inactive" but remains in the database.

This technique is useful in situations where it is necessary to keep a historical record of the data, but without it interfering with active operations.

6.2.2   Purge in non-Relational (NoSQL) databases.

In non-relational databases, such as MongoDB, Cassandra, or Redis, data purge can be more flexible due to the absence of rigid schemas.

These databases are designed to handle large volumes of unstructured and distributed data, allowing purge to be carried out more efficiently at scale.

Common techniques in NoSQL systems include the use of time-to-live (TTL), which is a mechanism that automatically sets the expiration of data after a specific period. This is useful in scenarios such as storing activity logs, where data is only relevant for a short period before being automatically purged.

Another technique is the use of data compression mechanisms, where old data is removed or aggregated into a more condensed format.

For example, in a database that stores measurements from IoT sensors, old data can be aggregated into monthly averages instead of keeping each individual reading.

6.3   Advantages and disadvantages of purging historical data.

While data purge is a necessary practice for the maintenance and efficiency of AI systems, it has both advantages and disadvantages that must be carefully weighed.

6.3.1   Advantages of purging.

1. Cost reduction.

    One of the main advantages of data purge is the reduction of storage and processing costs. By eliminating unnecessary data, organizations can save on infrastructure and improve the efficiency of systems, especially in big data environments.

2. Performance improvement.

    By reducing the amount of data stored, purge also improves the performance of data queries and analyses. This is particularly relevant in AI systems that rely on large volumes of data to make predictions and decisions in real time.

3. Regulatory compliance.

   Expungement is a key practice to ensure compliance with data protection regulations, such as GDPR and LGPD, which require the deletion of personal data when there is no longer justification for its storage.

6.3.2   Disadvantages of the purge.

1. Loss of History.

   The most obvious disadvantage of data purge is the loss of historical information that can be valuable for future analysis.

   Even if the data seems irrelevant at the moment, it can prove useful in future contexts, especially in areas such as scientific research and long-term trend analysis.

2. Risk of Undue Purge.

   If data purge is poorly implemented, there is a risk of eliminating data that is still relevant or necessary for future operations.

   This can hinder the ability of AI systems to perform thorough and accurate analysis.

6.4   Essential Data Preservation: How to determine what should not be purged.

The preservation of essential data is a necessary counterpoint to the purge process. To prevent the loss of critical information, organizations must adopt strict data retention policies that precisely determine what data should be kept and for how long.

Data retention policies should be based on a detailed analysis of the usefulness of the data, legal requirements, and the strategic needs of the organization.

A common approach is to categorize data according to its relevance to current and future operations, establishing specific retention periods for each category.

Data that is essential for historical analysis, regulatory compliance, or the development of new AI models should be preserved for a longer period of time.

A variety of tools and technologies are available to facilitate the preservation of critical data. Techniques such as data archiving, compression, and cloud storage offer efficient solutions to ensure that large volumes of data can be preserved for the long term without overloading operating systems.

These technologies allow data to be accessible when needed but stored in a way that minimizes the impact on the daily performance of systems.

6.5   Extensive preservation of historical data: a differentiated preservation.

Extensive preservation refers to the practice of collecting, storing, and maintaining data in an organized and accessible manner over time, with the goal of preserving it for future research, analysis, and uses.

6.5.1   Why is extensive preservation important?

- Digital historical heritage.

Digital historical data represents a valuable cultural and scientific heritage, which needs to be protected for future generations.

With a large amount of historical data available, AI systems can identify long-term patterns and make more accurate predictions.

- Search support.

Historical data can be used to conduct research in various areas of knowledge, such as history, sociology, economics, and natural sciences.

- Decision-making.

Historical information can serve as a basis for strategic decision-making in various areas, such as business, government, and urban planning.

- Legislation.

In some cases, the preservation of historical data is required by law, such as in the case of health or financial data.

Keeping a complete record of historical data ensures that the organization can respond to any requests or investigations that may arise in the future.

6.5.2   Challenges of preservation.

- Technological obsolescence.

Storage technologies and data formats evolve rapidly, making older data difficult to access and interpret.

Maintaining large volumes of historical data can negatively impact the performance of systems, especially if the data is not organized or accessed efficiently.

This can result in slower response times and greater complexity in data management.

- Volume of data.

The amount of data generated each day grows exponentially, requiring scalable and efficient storage solutions.

- Costs.

Data preservation requires investments in hardware, software, and specialized labor.

As data accumulates, infrastructure and maintenance expenses can increase significantly.

- Safety.

Historical data needs to be protected from loss, damage, and unauthorized access.

6.5.3   Strategies for preservation.

1. Choosing a robust database management system (DBMS). The DBMS must offer data backup, recovery, and replication functionalities.

2. Definition of a data retention policy. It is important to establish clear criteria for determining what data will be preserved and for how long.

3. Data migration. Data should be migrated periodically to new technologies to ensure its accessibility and integrity.

4. Metadata. It is essential to create detailed metadata about the data, describing its origin, format, content, and context.

5. Open file formats. Utilizing open file formats facilitates long-term preservation as it reduces reliance on specific software.

6. Regular backup. Performing frequent backups is essential to ensure data recovery in the event of failures.

While extensive data preservation has its advantages, it also presents challenges that must be considered when setting a retention policy.

6.6   Balancing purge and preservation.

Data purging and preservation are practices that, while opposed in their essence, must be balanced to ensure the efficiency, compliance, and relevance of AI systems.

While purging helps keep systems lean and efficient, preservation ensures that critical information is retained for future analysis and regulatory compliance.

When developing purge and preservation policies, it is critical for organizations to carefully consider their operational and strategic objectives, as well as legal requirements and industry best practices.

Only with a balanced approach can it be ensured that AI systems continue to operate effectively, making the most of the available data without overloading resources and without compromising the quality of analyses.

7 Between memory and time: parameters for the preservation of historical data.

Setting data retention policies is a critical aspect of information management in any organization, especially in contexts where Artificial Intelligence (AI) is used to process large volumes of historical data.

Effective data retention is not just a matter of storage, but involves strategic decisions about what information should be kept, for how long, and for what reasons.

7.1 Analysis of relevance and value of data.

The first step in defining data retention policies involves assessing the relevance and value of the data. This analysis should consider how data is utilized within the organization and its potential to contribute to future strategic decisions.

Data that is frequently accessed for analysis, reporting, or AI model development is more likely to be considered valuable and therefore should be kept for longer periods.

For example, in a financial institution, transactional data that covers an extended period of time can be essential for fraud detection and building predictive risk models.

In this case, prolonged retention of this data is justifiable. In contrast, temporary operational data, such as system logs, may have a shorter lifespan and may be scheduled for purge after a certain period, as discussed in the previous chapter.

7.2   Legal and Regulatory Considerations.

Data retention policies should also be aligned with relevant legal and regulatory requirements.

In many industries, regulations set minimum and maximum terms for the retention of certain types of data. For example, data protection legislation such as the GDPR in Europe and the LGPD in Brazil impose specific rules on how long personal information can be stored.

Additionally, industry regulations, such as those imposed by financial or health bodies, may require data retention for several years for auditing and compliance purposes. Failure to follow these guidelines can result in legal penalties and damage to the organization's reputation.

To implement effective retention policies, it is critical for organizations to develop clear strategies for data classification. This involves categorizing information based on its importance, sensitivity, and anticipated future use.

A common approach is to divide the data into categories such as:

- Critical data: information that is essential for continuous operation and strategic decision-making, which must be preserved for long periods of time.

- Regulatory data: data subject to specific legal requirements, which must be retained in accordance with established guidelines.

- Temporary data: information that has limited value in the short term and can be purged after a certain period of time.

Classifying data in this way allows organizations to enforce more accurate and efficient retention policies, balancing the need for preservation with data manageability.

Deciding which data to preserve and which to purge requires careful consideration of the costs and benefits involved.

Organizations must consider both the financial and operational impacts of their data preservation decisions, ensuring that the benefits outweigh the costs. This analysis should be revisited regularly as business needs and technologies evolve.

7.3   Tools and technologies for preserving historical data.

Effective preservation of historical data depends on adopting appropriate tools and technologies that can manage large volumes of information efficiently and securely.

Data archiving is a common practice for preserving information that is not accessed frequently but still needs to be retained for legal or strategic reasons.

Archiving tools allow data to be stored on lower-cost systems, freeing up space on primary operating systems.

Data compression is another important technique, especially in scenarios where storage space is a concern. Compression tools, such as lossless compression algorithms, reduce file sizes without compromising data integrity. This is particularly useful for preserving large volumes of historical data that must be kept for long periods.

Cloud storage has become a popular solution for preserving historical data, offering scalability, flexibility, and cost-effectiveness. Cloud providers, such as Amazon Web Services (AWS), Google Cloud Platform (GCP), and Microsoft Azure, offer a range of storage services that enable organizations to manage data in large volumes efficiently.

Using the cloud also makes it easier to implement archiving and backup strategies, ensuring that data is securely preserved and accessible when needed.

Additionally, cloud storage offers additional benefits such as geo-redundancy and disaster protection, which is crucial for ensuring business continuity.

Data lakes are another emerging solution for preserving large volumes of historical data.

Unlike Data Warehouses, which structure data in a rigid manner, data lakes allow for the storage of data in its raw, unstructured format, offering greater flexibility in how information is stored and accessed.

This flexibility is particularly useful in scenarios where historical data is generated in varying formats, such as server logs, IoT sensor streams, and multimedia files. With data lakes, organizations can store large amounts of data in a single repository, making it easy to analyze and integrate different types of data.

7.4   Use cases: When preservation is crucial.

While data preservation is a valuable practice in many contexts, there are specific situations where it becomes absolutely crucial. This segment examines use cases where preserving historical data not only adds value, but is essential to an organization's operation and success.

7.4.1   Preservation in health: longitudinality and disease prediction.

In the healthcare industry, preserving historical data plays a vital role in tracking patients over time and identifying disease patterns.

Longitudinal data, which records a patient's health trajectory over the years, is essential for personalizing treatments and epidemiological research.

For example, by analyzing historical patient data, researchers can identify risk factors for chronic diseases, allowing for early intervention and improved clinical outcomes.

The preservation of this data is also crucial for the prediction of disease outbreaks and for the elaboration of public health policies.

7.4.2   Finance: Risk Modeling and Trend Analysis

In the financial sector, the preservation of historical data is critical for risk modeling and the analysis of economic trends.

Historical data on transactions, market fluctuations, and consumer behavior provide the basis for predictive models that aid in strategic decision-making.

For example, banks and financial institutions use historical data to predict a customer's likelihood of default or to identify investment opportunities in emerging markets.

The ability to access and analyze this data over time is essential for staying competitive and compliant with financial regulations.

7.4.3 Education: Performance Evaluation and Learning Personalization

In the field of education, the preservation of historical data allows for the continuous evaluation of student performance and the personalization of learning experiences.

Historical data on student progress over time helps educators and administrators identify patterns of success and intervene early when difficulties arise.

Additionally, analyzing this data can inform the development of more effective curricula and pedagogical strategies by adjusting the content and pace of instruction to meet the individual needs of students.

8 The delicate balance: comparative analysis of historical data purge and preservation approaches.

Data purge is an essential practice for maintaining the efficiency and functionality of Artificial Intelligence (AI) systems, but its implementation involves complex and impactful decisions.

In this chapter, we will explore the different purge strategies, analyzing their practices and results, and comparing them with data preservation approaches.

8.1 Physical purge versus logical purge.

The first important distinction in the context of data purge is between physical purge and logical purge. Physical purge refers to the permanent removal of data from the system, resulting in an immediate release of storage space and a reduction in processing requirements.

This approach is straightforward and effective in scenarios where data is clearly stale and there is no need for additional retention.

On the other hand, logical purge involves marking data as "deleted" or "inactive," without physically removing it from the database.

This technique allows data to be recovered or reactivated if necessary, preserving the history of operations without directly affecting system performance.

However, logical purge can result in bloated databases, where large volumes of data marked as deleted continue to take up space and potentially impact performance.

8.2   Automatic versus manual purging.

Another crucial consideration is whether the purge is performed automatically or manually.

Automatic purge uses predefined rules to determine when and what data should be removed, ensuring ongoing maintenance and reducing the need for human intervention. This approach is useful in large-scale environments where the volume of data makes manual purge impractical.

However, manual purge gives you greater control and allows for more detailed analysis before data is removed. This is especially important in contexts where data may have a value that is not immediately apparent, or where regulatory compliance requires more careful analysis before purging.

However, manual purge is more susceptible to human error and can be less efficient, especially in systems that handle large volumes of data.

8.3   Effects of purge on performance.

Data purge can have a direct positive impact on the performance of AI systems. By reducing the amount of data that needs to be processed, indexed, and analyzed, purge improves query efficiency and processing speed.

This is especially important in systems that operate in real-time or that need to handle large volumes of data quickly and efficiently.

For example, in a recommendation system that uses user behavior data, removing records from inactive users or past interactions can speed up processing and improve the relevance of system-generated recommendations.

8.4   Ethical Considerations in Data Management.

In addition to legal issues, there are also ethical considerations involved in the decision to preserve or purge data. Preserving large volumes of personal data for long periods of time can raise concerns about privacy and misuse of that information.

Organizations have an ethical responsibility to ensure that data is used fairly and that the privacy of individuals is respected.

Data purging, on the other hand, can be seen as an ethical practice that promotes privacy and the protection of individuals' rights. However, it must also be carried out in a transparent and responsible manner, ensuring that data that still has value or is necessary for legal compliance is not improperly removed.

8.5   Emerging innovations and future approaches.

With the continuous evolution of technology, new innovations are emerging to help organizations better manage the balance between purge and data preservation.

These innovations are redefining the way data is stored, managed, and accessed, providing new opportunities to optimize the efficiency of AI systems.

Cloud computing has transformed the way organizations handle large volumes of data. Distributed storage allows data to be stored redundantly in different geographic locations, providing greater resiliency and accessibility.

This is particularly useful for the preservation of historical data, allowing large amounts of information to be maintained without compromising the performance of systems.

Additionally, cloud solutions offer on-demand scalability, allowing organizations to adjust their storage resources as needed, without the need for significant investments in physical infrastructure.

8.6   Artificial intelligence for data management.

AI itself is being used to optimize the data management process. AI-powered tools can automatically analyze large volumes of data to identify what information should be preserved and what can be purged.

These systems can learn from the organization's usage patterns and needs by adjusting purge and preservation policies in real time.

This AI-powered approach offers a dynamic solution to the dilemma between purging and preservation, allowing organizations to maintain the right balance between efficiency and retention of valuable information.

9 Global regulatory compliance in the preservation of historical data.

In an increasingly connected world, global organizations face the challenge of complying with a vast array of data protection and records preservation regulations that vary significantly between different jurisdictions.

These regulations, while sharing common goals of protecting privacy and data integrity, have substantial differences in terms of specific requirements, penalties for non-compliance, and enforcement approaches.

This chapter explores the key international regulations that impact the preservation of historical data, offering a detailed comparison between Europe's General Data Protection Regulation (GDPR), Brazil's General Data Protection Law (LGPD), California's Consumer Privacy Act (CCPA), and other relevant laws. At the end, strategies for global organizations to navigate this complex regulatory landscape will be discussed.

9.1 GDPR (General Data Protection Regulation) – Europe.

The GDPR, which came into effect on May 25, 2018, is one of the most comprehensive and influential data protection regulations in the world. It applies to all organizations that process personal data of European Union (EU) residents, regardless of where the organization is located.

The GDPR imposes strict rules on the retention of personal data, requiring that data be kept only for as long as necessary for the purposes for which it was collected. After this period, the data must be deleted or anonymized in an irreversible manner.

Relevant Articles:

Article 5: Data protection principles, including storage limitation (Article 5.1(e)), which requires the deletion of data when it is no longer needed.

Article 17: Right to be forgotten, which allows individuals to request the deletion of their personal data when there is no legal need to keep it.

GDPR is known for its severe penalties, which can be as high as €20 million or 4% of the organization's annual global turnover, whichever is greater. These fines highlight the importance of strict compliance.

9.2   LGPD (General Data Protection Law) – Brazil.

Inspired by the GDPR, the LGPD came into force on September 18, 2020 and aims to protect the fundamental rights of freedom and privacy, in addition to regulating the processing of personal data in Brazil.

The law applies to any personal data processing operation carried out by a natural person or by a legal entity, under public or private law, regardless of the medium, the country of headquarters or the country where the data is located.

Like the GDPR, the LGPD requires that personal data be kept only for as long as necessary to fulfill its purposes. After the end of this period, the data must be deleted or anonymized.

Relevant Articles:

Article 15: Establishes that the termination of data processing will occur when the purpose has been achieved or when the data is no longer necessary or relevant for the achievement of the specific purpose.

Article 18: Guarantees data subjects the right to request the deletion of their personal data, except when there is legal justification for its maintenance.

Penalties for non-compliance with the LGPD may include warnings, fines of up to 2% of the company's revenue in Brazil (limited to BRL 50 million per infraction), blocking of the personal data to which the infraction refers until its regularization, and even the deletion of personal data.

8.4. CCPA (California Consumer Privacy Act) - California, USA.

The CCPA, which went into effect on January 1, 2020, is one of the strictest privacy regulations in the United States. It gives California residents greater control over how their personal information is collected and used, applying to businesses that collect data from California residents and that meet certain revenue or data volume criteria.

While the CCPA does not have data retention requirements as specific as the GDPR and LGPD, it does impose transparency obligations and gives consumers the right to request deletion of their personal information.

Relevant Sections:

Section 1798.105: Right to request deletion, which allows consumers to request that a business delete any personal information it collects, subject to certain exceptions.

Section 1798.110: Requires businesses to inform consumers about the categories of personal information being collected and the purposes for which that information is used.

Penalties for violating the CCPA can include fines of up to $7,500 for willful violation and $2,500 for non-willful violation, as well as allowing consumers to seek civil damages in certain circumstances.

9.3   Other relevant regulations.

In addition to the three main regulations discussed, other jurisdictions also have their own data protection and records preservation laws that are worth mentioning.

9.3.1   PIPEDA (Personal Information Protection and Electronic Documents Act) – Canada.

Overview.

PIPEDA regulates the collection, use, and disclosure of personal information in Canada, applying to the private sector. It requires organizations to obtain consent for the collection of personal data and to protect that data adequately.

Preservation Requirements.

PIPEDA does not specify data retention periods, but requires that personal data be retained only for as long as it is necessary to fulfill the purposes for which it was collected.

Penalties.

Non-compliance with PIPEDA may result in investigations and corrective actions by the Privacy Commissioner, as well as potential lawsuits by affected individuals.

9.3.2   Indian Personal Data Protection Bill.

Overview.

India is in the process of implementing a new data protection legislation that resembles the GDPR. The bill establishes rules for the collection, storage, and processing of personal data.

Preservation Requirements.

The bill requires that personal data be retained only for as long as necessary for the purposes for which it was collected, and subsequently be deleted.

Penalties.

Proposed penalties include fines of up to 4% of the organization's annual global turnover for serious violations.

9.4   Comparison of international regulations.

The following is a detailed comparison of the key aspects of the regulations discussed:

Regulação	Âmbito de Aplicação	Requisitos de Preservação de Dados	Direito de Exclusão	Penalidades Máximas
GDPR	União Europeia	Retenção limitada ao tempo necessário para as finalidades	Direito ao esquecimento (Art. 17)	Até 20 milhões de euros ou 4% do faturamento global
LGPD	Brasil	Retenção limitada ao tempo necessário para as finalidades	Direito de exclusão (Art. 18)	Até 2% do faturamento, limitado a R$ 50 milhões
CCPA	Califórnia, EUA	Foco em transparência e consentimento	Direito de exclusão (Seção 1798.105)	Até $7.500 por violação intencional
PIPEDA	Canadá	Retenção enquanto necessário para as finalidades	Não especificado	Penalidades civis e ações corretivas
Lei de Proteção de Dados da Índia	Índia	Retenção limitada ao tempo necessário para as finalidades ↓	Direito de exclusão	Até 4% do faturamento global

Given the differences in international regulations, global organizations need to adopt robust strategies to ensure compliance in different markets.

Here are some recommendations:

- Organizations should develop a global data protection policy that can be tailored to meet the specific requirements of each jurisdiction. This includes implementing data consent, retention, and deletion processes that are flexible and can be adjusted as needed.

- Designate Data Protection Officers (DPOs) in each region or country where the organization operates. These DPOs will be responsible for monitoring compliance with local laws and coordinating with global teams to ensure a harmonized approach.

- Invest in automation tools to manage deletion requests, compliance audits, and data protection impact reporting. This can include using AI technologies to detect and remediate potential breaches before they occur.

- Promote an ongoing training program for employees on relevant data protection regulations and best practices to ensure compliance. Awareness is a key component of avoiding mistakes that could lead to breaches.

Complying with international data protection regulations is a complex but essential challenge for organizations operating in a global marketplace.

Compliance not only protects organizations from severe penalties but also builds trust with customers and stakeholders by demonstrating a commitment to privacy and data protection.

By taking a strategic and proactive approach, organizations can successfully navigate the different regulations and ensure that their historical data is managed securely, ethically, and in compliance with applicable laws.

10 International Organization for Standardization (ISO) and standards related to the management and preservation of historical data.

The International Organization for Standardization (ISO), founded in 1947, is a non-governmental and independent organization that develops and publishes international standards.

ISO is headquartered in Geneva, Switzerland, and operates in more than 160 countries, bringing together experts to create standards that ensure quality, safety, and efficiency in various sectors, including information technology, health, safety, environment, and management.

ISO standards are widely recognized and adopted globally, and serve as a benchmark to ensure that products, services, and systems are consistent, safe, and of high quality.

In the context of the management and preservation of historical data, ISO offers a series of standards that, although not specifically targeted at historical data, provide essential guidelines for the security, archiving and management of information.

10.1   ISO/IEC 27001: Information Security Management.

ISO/IEC 27001 is an internationally recognized standard for information security management.

First published in 2005 and revised in 2013 and 2022, this standard establishes requirements for the creation, implementation, maintenance, and continuous improvement of an Information Security Management System (ISMS).

ISO/IEC 27001 has as its main objective to protect the confidentiality, integrity, and availability of information in organizations. This is achieved through the implementation of security controls that are constantly monitored, evaluated, and improved.

The standard is applicable to any organization, regardless of its size or industry, and is especially relevant to those that handle sensitive information, such as personal data or critical historical data.

ISO/IEC 27001 follows the High-Level Structure (HLS) common to ISO management system standards, which facilitates integration with other management systems, such as ISO 9001 (Quality) and ISO 14001 (Environment).

The standard is organized into 10 main clauses, the most relevant of which are for the management of historical data:

- Clause 4: Context of the Organization: requires the organization to understand the context in which it operates, including the expectations of stakeholders and the applicable legal requirements.

- Clause 6: Planning: includes the assessment of risks and opportunities related to information security, as well as the establishment of objectives and controls for risk mitigation.

- Clause 8: Operation: focuses on the implementation and operation of the ISMS, including change control and security incident management.

- Clause 9: Performance Evaluation: deals with the monitoring, measurement, analysis and evaluation of the ISMS, ensuring that it remains effective and adequate over time.

- Clause 10: Improvement: emphasizes the continuous improvement of the management system to adapt to new threats and challenges.

ISO/IEC 27001 is highly relevant to historical data management, as it ensures that information is protected from unauthorized access, corruption, and loss.

The standard helps organizations establish robust policies and procedures for data preservation while minimizing the risks associated with managing large volumes of information over time. Implementing an ISMS based on ISO/IEC 27001 ensures that historical data is kept in a secure and controlled environment.

10.2 ISO 14721: OAIS (Open Archival Information System) Reference Model.

ISO 14721, better known as OAIS (Open Archival Information System), is a standard that provides a reference model for the long-term preservation of digital information.

First published in 2003 and revised in 2012, OAIS was developed for institutions that need to ensure that digital information is preserved and accessible for long periods.

The OAIS defines a reference model that describes the roles and responsibilities of a digital archiving system.

It does not prescribe specific implementations, but provides a conceptual framework that can be adapted to a wide variety of contexts, including archives, libraries, museums, and other institutions dealing with digital preservation.

The OAIS is composed of six main functions:

- Ingest: refers to the process of acquiring digital information for the archiving system. It includes data reception, compliance validation, and initial storage.

- Data Storage (Archival Storage): involves the physical and logical management of the stored information, ensuring its preservation over time.

- Data Management: focuses on maintaining the metadata that describes the archived data, allowing its future retrieval and interpretation.

- Administration: Involves the management of the archiving system, including preservation policies, backup strategies, and regulatory compliance.

- Preservation Planning: refers to the creation of strategies to ensure the long-term accessibility of digital information, including the migration of formats and adaptation to new technologies.

- Access: Addresses the dissemination of archived information, ensuring that users can locate, access, and interpret the preserved data.

OAIS is widely used in industries that require the preservation of large volumes of digital historical data, such as digital libraries and government archives.

It offers a solid framework to ensure that historical data is preserved with integrity, authenticity, and accessibility over time.

Organizations that implement an OAIS-based system can ensure that their historical data remains useful and interpretable, even decades after its creation.

10.3   ISO 15489: Document Management.

ISO 15489 is the most recognized international standard for document management, establishing principles and practices for creating, capturing, maintaining, and disposing of documents and records in any format.

First published in 2001 and revised in 2016, the standard is widely adopted in industries that require strict document management, such as governments, financial institutions, and large corporations.

ISO 15489 aims to ensure that documents are managed efficiently and effectively throughout their entire lifecycle, from creation to destruction or permanent archiving.

The standard is applicable to all types of documents and establishes guidelines to ensure that records are authentic, reliable, complete, and usable.

ISO 15489 is divided into two parts:

- Part 1: Concepts and Principles: This section defines the fundamental concepts and principles of document management, including the need to create authentic and reliable records that can serve as evidence of activities and transactions.

- Part 2: Guidelines: This section provides practical guidelines for implementing a document management system, including capturing, classifying, storing, accessing, and deleting records.

The principles set out by ISO 15489 include:

- Authenticity: Documents must be protected from unauthorized alteration to ensure that they accurately represent the activities they document.

- Reliability: Documents should be created and maintained in a way that can be trusted as evidence of transactions.

- Integrity: Documents must be complete and free of corruption.

- Usefulness: Documents should be accessible and understandable to those who need to use them.

ISO 15489 is particularly relevant to historical data management, as it provides a framework for ensuring that records are managed in a way that preserves their authenticity, integrity, and accessibility.

In the context of AI and big data, the standard can be applied to ensure that historical data used for training and analysis is properly managed, ensuring the quality and reliability of the results.

10.4   ISO 16363: Auditing and certification of trusted digital repositories.

ISO 16363 is a standard that defines the requirements for the auditing and certification of trusted digital repositories, ensuring that they meet the standards necessary for the long-term preservation of digital data.

Published in 2012, this standard is based on the OAIS model and expands its guidelines to provide specific criteria for the evaluation of digital repositories.

The goal of ISO 16363 is to ensure that digital repositories are able to reliably preserve digital data over time while maintaining the authenticity, integrity, and accessibility of the information.

The standard establishes specific criteria for evaluating the reliability of a digital repository, covering technical, organizational, and governance aspects.

ISO 16363 is organized around three main areas:

Organization and Management: evaluates the organizational structure, governance, and policies of a digital repository. This includes the existence of clear digital preservation policies, a qualified team, and the financial capacity to sustain the repository in the long term.

Digital Object Management: focuses on the technical processes for managing digital objects, including data ingestion, storage, preservation and access. The standard evaluates the repository's ability to maintain the integrity and authenticity of digital objects.

Technological and Security Infrastructure: evaluates the technological infrastructure of the repository, including hardware, software, and security systems. The standard examines the repository's ability to protect data from loss, corruption, and unauthorized access.

ISO 16363 is especially relevant for organizations that need to ensure the preservation of historical data in trusted digital repositories. By following the guidelines of the standard, organizations can obtain certification that their repositories meet the highest standards of reliability, ensuring that historical data is preserved securely and affordably in the long term.

10.5   ISO/IEC 27040: Security of information storage.

ISO/IEC 27040 is a standard that provides guidelines for the security of information storage, addressing best practices for protecting data at rest from internal and external threats.

Published in 2015, the standard is an extension of the ISO/IEC 27000 set of standards for information security.

ISO/IEC 27040 aims to help organizations protect their stored data from loss, corruption, unauthorized access, and other threats.

The standard addresses security in different types of storage, including networked storage systems (NAS), cloud storage, and local storage devices.

ISO/IEC 27040 provides comprehensive guidelines for protecting data at rest, including:

- Encryption: recommends encrypting sensitive data to protect against unauthorized access and ensure confidentiality.

- Access Controls: suggests implementing strict access controls to ensure that only authorized people can access the stored data.

- Key Management: emphasizes the importance of effective cryptographic key management to ensure that encrypted data can be recovered securely.

- Backup and Recovery: Provides guidance for implementing backup and disaster recovery strategies, ensuring that data can be restored in the event of loss or corruption.

- Physical Security: addresses the need to physically protect storage devices from theft, damage, or interference.

ISO/IEC 27040 is highly relevant to the preservation of historical data, as it ensures that stored data is protected from threats and remains accessible and healthy over time.

Applying the security guidelines of the standard helps organizations mitigate the risks associated with storing large volumes of historical data, protecting it from unauthorized access and other threats.

10.6   The relevance of ISO standards in historical data management.

The ISO standards discussed in this annex offer a comprehensive set of guidelines and best practices for the management and preservation of historical data.

While each standard has a specific focus, together, they provide a solid foundation for ensuring that historical data is managed securely, efficiently, and in accordance with international best practices.

Implementing these standards not only helps organizations comply with regulations and protect their data, but also maximizes the value of historical data in their AI systems by ensuring that this data can be utilized for accurate insights and informed decisions in the long term.

Adhering to ISO standards is a best practice for any organization dealing with large volumes of historical data, as it ensures that this data is preserved with integrity and accessibility, contributing to the continued success of its AI-powered operations and strategies.

11 Future trends and innovations in the treatment of historical data.

Effective management of historical data has been a constant challenge as organizations deal with ever-increasing volumes of information. However, new technologies are emerging to transform the way this data is stored, processed, and used.

These innovations are shaping the future of Artificial Intelligence (AI), allowing organizations to maintain a complete and detailed view of their data history, without sacrificing efficiency or scalability.

One of the most significant trends is the use of AI itself to manage data retention policies. Machine learning algorithms can analyze data usage patterns and automatically determine which information is essential for preservation and which can be purged without harm.

For example, an AI system can monitor how different datasets are utilized in predictive models, identifying which data is frequently accessed and which have little to no impact on the model's performance.

Based on this analysis, AI can suggest or even automatically perform the purge of irrelevant data, optimizing system performance and reducing storage costs.

Another emerging trend is a focus on the data lifecycle, where organizations develop retention policies that consider the entire lifecycle of data, from its creation to its eventual purge.

This includes continuously analyzing the value of data over time and implementing archiving and purge strategies that reflect that value.

By taking a data lifecycle-based approach, organizations can ensure that data is retained while it has operational value and disposed of securely and efficiently when it is no longer needed.

This holistic approach helps balance the need for preservation with the demands of performance and compliance.

As AI technologies continue to evolve, preserving historical data will face new challenges and open up new opportunities. This segment explores what the future holds for historical data management in AI and how organizations can prepare for these changes.

The volume of data generated globally is growing at an exponential rate, driven by technologies such as the Internet of Things (IoT), social media, and big data.

This growth puts enormous pressure on storage and processing infrastructures, requiring innovative solutions to ensure that historical data can be preserved and accessed efficiently.

Organizations will need to adopt more advanced storage technologies, such as high-density hard drives, optical storage, and even new DNA-based storage approaches, which promise nearly unlimited capacity on a very small physical scale.

In a broader sense, AI also has the potential to play a key role in preserving society's collective memories by archiving and making accessible large volumes of historical data that reflect human culture, history, and knowledge. This includes digitizing and preserving libraries, media files, and historical records.

AI can help organize, index, and make available these vast collections of data, ensuring that future generations have access to humanity's accumulated memories and knowledge.

The future of historical data management is full of exciting possibilities and complex challenges. Organizations that want to prepare for this future must adopt a strategic approach that takes advantage of emerging technological innovations while mitigating the associated risks.

12 Conclusion.

Throughout this book, we have explored in detail the various facets of historical data management in Artificial Intelligence (AI) systems, addressing both preservation techniques and purge strategies.

In this final section, we will review the main challenges and limitations that arose in the previous discussions, offering a critical view and a synthesis of the lessons learned.

The technical challenges in managing historical data are vast and varied, ranging from the scalability of storage systems to the complexity of querying and analyzing large volumes of data.

The exponential growth of data, driven by the proliferation of IoT devices, social networks, and other sources of big data, creates continuous pressure on organizations' technological infrastructure.

Another significant challenge is maintaining data integrity and temporal consistency. In distributed systems, ensuring that historical data is accurate and consistent over time requires advanced synchronization and versioning techniques, as well as robust validation and auditing policies.

Historical data management is not just a technical issue, but also involves ethical and legal considerations that must be carefully weighed. Data protection regulations, such as the GDPR and LGPD, impose strict requirements on the retention, purge, and use of personal data, requiring organizations to implement policies that protect the privacy of individuals and prevent the misuse of sensitive information.

Additionally, there are ethical issues surrounding fairness and fairness in the use of historical data in AI systems. Bias in data can perpetuate inequalities and social injustices, especially in contexts where algorithmic decisions have a significant impact on people's lives.

The ethical responsibility of organizations includes not only compliance with laws, but also careful consideration of the social implications of their data management practices.

Historical data plays a key role in the development and operation of AI systems. As technology advances, the importance of this data is only likely to grow, shaping the future of AI in profound and lasting ways.

AI is constantly evolving, and this transformation is driven by data. The more data an AI can access and learn, the more sophisticated and accurate its predictive capabilities become.

However, this reliance on historical data also brings with it challenges, such as the need to ensure that models remain relevant in an ever-changing world.

The use of historical data will continue to be essential for the continuous improvement of AI models. They provide the context needed to understand trends and patterns over time, allowing AIs to make more accurate predictions and make more informed decisions.

Emerging trends, such as the use of AI to automate data management, the adoption of more advanced storage technologies, and the development of new temporal analytics frameworks, are shaping the future of historical data management.

Innovations such as blockchain to ensure data immutability and storage in DNA for nearly limitless capabilities are on the horizon, promising to radically transform the way historical data is preserved and utilized.

Organizations looking to position themselves at the forefront of technology must be aware of these trends and ready to adopt new approaches that can optimize their data management and improve the effectiveness of their AI systems.

The use of historical data in AI has the potential to perpetuate inequalities and injustices if not carefully managed. It is essential for organizations to consider the social impact of their data management practices and work to ensure that their AIs are developed and operated in an ethical and responsible manner.

This includes recognizing biases in data, implementing measures to mitigate those biases, and committing to transparency and accountability in automated decisions.

Organizations should strive to create AI systems that promote justice, equity, and social well-being while avoiding practices that could cause harm or exclusion.

The future of historical data management is fraught with challenges, such as the continued growth of data, changing regulations, and the need to maintain operational efficiency. However, there are also numerous opportunities for innovation and improvement, from using AI to automate data management to exploring new storage technologies.

Organizations that can balance these challenges with emerging opportunities will be well-positioned to make the most of their historical data, ensuring that their AI systems remain effective, ethical, and accountable.

Careful preservation of historical data, balanced with the need for efficiency and relevance, will enable organizations to build AI systems that not only respond to today's demands, but are also capable of meeting tomorrow's challenges.

As I close this book, I invite the reader to reflect on their role in this ever-evolving field. Whether you're an IT manager, a data scientist, a regulator, or an academic, the role you play in preserving historical data is crucial to the continued success of your organization and society as a whole.

This book is part of Prof. Marcão's Artificial Intelligence Collection, with 49 volumes, it is a series dedicated to exploring the complexities and implications of AI in contemporary society.

Available on Amazon, the collection offers an in-depth and critical look at the role of data, information, and knowledge in the age of artificial intelligence, serving as an indispensable resource for professionals, academics, and enthusiasts in the field.

13 Glossary.

This glossary is designed to assist readers in understanding the specific technical terms and concepts used throughout the book. The management and preservation of historical data in Artificial Intelligence (AI) systems involves terminologies that, for many, may be complex or unknown.

This glossary serves as a quick and useful reference to clarify these terms, providing a more fluid and informed reading.

1   Anonymization. The process of transforming personal data in such a way that the individuals to whom this data refers can no longer be identified, directly or indirectly, reducing privacy risks.

2   API (Application Programming Interface). A set of definitions and protocols that allows different software to communicate with each other. In the context of AI, APIs can be used to integrate data preservation and management functionalities with other systems.

3   Cloud Storage. Method of storing data on remote servers accessible via the internet. The data is kept on a network of servers managed by a cloud service provider, allowing for remote access and scalability.

4   Big Data. Extremely large and complex datasets that are difficult to process and analyze using traditional methods. Big Data is a crucial source of information for AI systems, especially in model training.

5   Blockchain. Distributed ledger technology that stores information in connected blocks on a chain, ensuring the immutability of data. Used to preserve the integrity and transparency of historical data.

6   Data Lifecycle. Set of stages through which data passes, from its creation to its eventual elimination. It includes the capture, storage, use, archiving, and purging of the data.

7   Regulatory Compliance. Adherence to relevant laws, regulations, guidelines, and specifications governing data protection and use. Regulatory compliance is critical to ensuring legality and security in data management.

8   Cryptography. Information encoding process to prevent unauthorized access. In preserving historical data, encryption ensures that the stored data is secure and accessible only to authorized people.

9   Data Governance. A set of practices and policies that ensure that data is managed securely, efficiently, and in accordance with legal and regulatory requirements. Data governance is essential for the integrity and quality of historical data.

10 Data Mining. Process of discovering patterns and useful information from large data sets. In AI, data mining can be used to extract valuable insights from historical data.

11 Deduplication. Data compression technique that eliminates redundant copies of information, saving storage space. Often used in data backup and archiving systems.

12 Data Purge. The process of securely and permanently removing data that is no longer needed or has reached the end of its lifecycle. Purge helps maintain the efficiency and compliance of data storage systems.

13 Scalability. Ability of a system, network, or process to handle an increased load without compromising performance. In the context of data preservation, scalability is essential to managing growing volumes of historical data.

14 Fairness Constraints. Constraints built into AI models to ensure that results are fair and non-discriminatory. These constraints are especially important in contexts where biases in historical data can affect automated decisions.

15 Framework. A framework or set of tools and libraries that facilitate the development and implementation of software systems, including AI and data management systems.

16 GDPR (General Data Protection Regulation). European Data Protection Regulation that sets strict rules on how organizations should handle personal data. The GDPR is a milestone in privacy protection and is relevant to any organization that handles data from residents of the European Union.

17 Data Governance. Set of practices and policies to ensure that data is managed securely, efficiently and in accordance with legal requirements. It involves defining responsibilities, processes, and controls for data management.

18 Hashing. Process of transforming input data of any length into a fixed-length string, using a hash function. Hashing is widely used to ensure data integrity and to protect sensitive information.

19 Data Heterogeneity. It refers to the variety of formats, sources, and types of data that need to be managed in an AI system. Data heterogeneity can include text, images, videos, structured and unstructured data.

20 AI (Artificial Intelligence). A field of computer science that develops systems capable of performing tasks that normally require human intelligence, such as speech recognition, computer vision, and decision-making. AI is widely applied in the analysis and management of historical data.

21 Immutability. Ownership of something that cannot be changed or modified. In technology, immutability often refers to data or records that, once recorded, cannot be modified, such as in a blockchain system.

22 Data Integration. The process of combining data from different sources to provide a unified view. Data integration is crucial for analyzing historical data that comes from multiple sources.

23 Journaling. A data preservation technique where a record of all transactions affecting a dataset is kept. Journaling ensures that in the event of a failure, data can be restored to its previous state.

24 Key Management. Process of managing cryptographic keys in a security system, essential to ensure that encrypted data can be accessed and decrypted only by authorized users.

25 KPI (Key Performance Indicator). Metrics used to assess an organization's success in achieving specific objectives. In the context of AI, KPIs can be used to measure the performance of data preservation models and systems.

26 LGPD (General Data Protection Law). Brazilian data protection legislation, inspired by the European GDPR, which regulates the collection, processing, and storage of personal data in Brazil.

27 Data Longevity. Ability of data to be retained in an accessible and usable format over time. Data longevity is a key consideration in preserving historical data.

28 Metadata. Data that describes other data, providing information such as origin, format, author, and date of creation. Metadata is essential for organizing and retrieving historical data.

29 Data Migration. The process of transferring data from one system or format to another. Data migration is necessary to ensure that historical data remains accessible as technologies evolve.

30 Network-Attached Storage (NAS). A storage device connected to a network that allows access by multiple users and systems. NAS is widely used for centralized data storage in organizations.

31 OAIS (Open Archival Information System). Reference model for a digital archiving system, widely used for the long-term preservation of digital information. OAIS is an international standard that ensures the continuous accessibility of data over time.

32 Technological obsolescence. A situation in which a technology or system becomes obsolete and is no longer supported or used. In data preservation, technological obsolescence is a risk that must be managed to ensure continued access to data.

33 Pseudonymization. A data processing technique in which personal identifiers are replaced by pseudonyms, reducing the risk of identifying individuals but allowing data analysis.

34 Data Protection. Set of practices, processes, and technologies to protect data from unauthorized access, loss, corruption, and other threats. Data protection is essential to ensure the privacy and security of information.

35 Data Quality. Measure of how well the data meets the needs of its users. Data quality is determined by factors such as accuracy, completeness, consistency, and timeliness.

36 Data Quarantine. The process of isolating potentially corrupted or infected data to prevent it from affecting other systems or data. Data quarantine is a common practice in information security systems.

37 Data Redundancy. The existence of multiple copies of data in different locations or systems, used as a security measure to prevent data loss in the event of a system failure. Redundancy is crucial to ensure the integrity of historical data.

38 Trusted Digital Repository. Data storage system that meets specific criteria of security, integrity and accessibility, ensuring the long-term preservation of data. Trusted digital repositories are certified by standards such as ISO 16363.

39 Information Security. A set of practices and technologies used to protect information from unauthorized access, misuse, disclosure, alteration, or destruction. Information security is a key consideration in historical data management.

40 SLA (Service Level Agreement). Service level agreement between a service provider and a customer, which defines the expected levels of service, such as response time, availability, and support. SLAs are important to ensure that data storage and management services meet customer expectations.

41 Tokenization. The process of replacing sensitive data with non-sensitive identifiers, called tokens, that can be used in systems without exposing the original data. Tokenization is used to protect data during processing.

42 Fault tolerance. Ability of a system to continue to operate correctly even when a part of its component fails. Data storage and preservation systems must have high fault tolerance to ensure continued access to historical data.

43 Storage Unit. A device or system used to store data digitally, such as hard drives, SSDs, NAS systems, or cloud solutions. The choice of storage unit depends on capacity, speed, and security requirements.

44 Use of Data. The use of data to achieve specific objectives, such as analysis, decision-making, or reporting. The effective use of data depends on the quality and accessibility of the data stored.

45 Data biases. Inequities or distortions in data that can lead to unfair or incorrect results in AI models. Mitigating bias is crucial to ensure the fairness and accuracy of automated decisions.

46 Data Virtualization. A technique for creating a virtual layer that allows access to data from multiple sources as if it were from a single source. Virtualization makes it easier to integrate and use historical data stored in different systems.

47 Web Scraping. A technique of automatic data extraction from websites, used to collect information for analysis. Web scraping is a common source of unstructured data that can be integrated into historical analytics.

48 Workload. The workload or volume of tasks that a data processing system must perform. Workload management is important for maintaining the performance and efficiency of AI systems.

49 XML (Extensible Markup Language). Markup language used to define data formatting rules, allowing data to be shared and interpreted in a consistent manner between different systems. XML is widely used in data storage and exchange.

50 Yottabyte. A unit of measurement for data storage equivalent to 1 trillion terabytes (TB) or 1,000 zettabytes (ZB). Yottabyte is used to describe extremely large volumes of data, which are common in big data and AI.

51 Zero-Knowledge Proof. A cryptographic protocol that allows one party to prove to another that a statement is true, without revealing any information other than the veracity of the statement. Used in security systems to protect data privacy.

52 Zettabyte. A unit of measurement for data storage equivalent to 1 billion terabytes (TB) or 1,000 exabytes (EB). The zettabyte is a relevant measure in the context of big data and historical data storage.

14 FAQ.

1   What is historical data preservation?

Historical data preservation refers to the process of maintaining and protecting information that has long-term value, ensuring that it remains accessible, usable, and healthy over time.

This involves secure storage, proper management, and protection against technological loss, corruption, or obsolescence.

2   Why is the preservation of historical data important for Artificial Intelligence (AI)?

Historical data is crucial for training AI models, as it provides the necessary context for learning and predicting future patterns.

The quality and integrity of this data directly influences the accuracy and effectiveness of AI systems.

Additionally, preserving this data allows for longitudinal analysis that can reveal important trends and insights over time.

3   What are the key regulations that affect the preservation of historical data?

Key regulations include the GDPR (General Data Protection Regulation) in Europe, the LGPD (General Data Protection Law) in Brazil, and the CCPA (California Consumer Privacy Act) in California, USA.

These regulations establish guidelines on how personal data should be collected, stored, used, and eventually eliminated, as well as imposing compliance and security requirements.

4   How does regulatory compliance impact the preservation of historical data?

Regulatory compliance imposes obligations on how personal data is managed, including retention and purge.

Organizations need to ensure that historical data is preserved in accordance with legal requirements, which may include anonymizing or deleting data when it is no longer needed.

Non-compliance can result in severe penalties in addition to reputational damage.

5   What is the difference between cloud storage and DNA storage for historical data?

Cloud storage is a widely used technology that allows the storage of large volumes of data on remote servers, accessible via the internet.

It offers scalability and global accessibility. DNA storage is an emerging technology that uses the structure of DNA to store data at an extremely high density, with the advantage of offering significant longevity.

However, DNA storage is still experimental and much more expensive compared to cloud storage.

6   How can blockchain be used in the preservation of historical data?

Blockchain can be used to ensure the integrity and immutability of historical data.

Each transaction or data change is recorded in a block, which is then added to a chain (blockchain), creating an immutable and transparent record.

This is particularly useful in scenarios where it is crucial to ensure that data is not altered or manipulated, such as in public records, legal documents, and histories.

7   What are fairness constraints in AI and why are they important?

Fairness constraints are mechanisms built into AI models to ensure that automated decisions are fair and unbiased.

These restrictions are important because they help mitigate bias in historical data, which can lead to discriminatory or unfair outcomes. Implementing equity constraints is critical to ensuring that AI systems promote social justice and equity.

8   What does "data purge" mean and when should it be performed?

Data purge refers to the process of securely and permanently erasing data that is no longer needed or has reached the end of its lifecycle.

The purge should be carried out in compliance with data retention policies and applicable regulations, often when the data no longer has legal, operational, or analytical value to the organization.

9   What are the key emerging technologies in preserving historical data?

Some of the key emerging technologies include DNA storage, which offers an extremely high storage density and significant longevity; blockchain, which guarantees the integrity and immutability of data; and Artificial Intelligence, which can be used to automate data management, identify patterns in large volumes of historical data, and improve preservation accuracy.

10   How does technological obsolescence affect the preservation of historical data?

Technological obsolescence occurs when data formats, systems, or technologies become outdated and are no longer supported. This can make it difficult to access historical data or make it completely inaccessible.

To mitigate this risk, organizations must implement data migration strategies, keeping data in up-to-date formats and transferring it to new platforms as technology evolves.

11   What are the ethical challenges in preserving historical data?

Ethical challenges include ensuring the privacy of individuals, avoiding the perpetuation of historical biases in AI models, and balancing the need for preservation with the right to be forgotten.

Organizations should carefully consider the ethical implications of their data preservation practices, ensuring that decisions are made fairly and responsibly.

12   How can organizations ensure the longevity of historical data?

To ensure the longevity of historical data, organizations should adopt robust preservation practices, such as utilizing durable data formats, implementing redundancy and regular backups, and migrating data to new technologies as needed.

Additionally, it is essential to maintain detailed documentation and complete metadata to ensure that the data can be interpreted and used in the future.

13   What are the best practices for historical data governance?

Best practices include creating clear data retention and purge policies, implementing strict access controls, utilizing automation tools for data governance, and conducting regular audits to ensure compliance and data integrity.

Effective governance ensures that historical data is managed securely, efficiently, and in compliance with regulations.

14   How can AI improve the preservation of historical data?

Artificial Intelligence can be used to automate many of the tasks involved in preserving historical data, such as detecting patterns, analyzing data integrity, and identifying redundant or unnecessary data.

Additionally, AI can help predict future preservation issues and suggest mitigation strategies, making the process more efficient and accurate.

15   How can organizations deal with the different regulatory requirements in multiple jurisdictions?

Global organizations must take a strategic approach to regulatory compliance by developing global data protection policies that can be tailored to meet the specific requirements of each jurisdiction.

This includes designating data protection officers in each region, automating compliance processes, and conducting ongoing training to ensure that all employees are aware of applicable regulations.

15 References.

ANTHROPIC. (2023). Claude AI: An Introduction. Anthropic Research Publication.

ARMSTRONG, M., & MARSTON, S. (2020). Cloud Storage: A Comprehensive Guide to Managing Data in the Cloud. Journal of Cloud Computing, 8(1), 1-22.

BAROCAS, S., & SELBST, A. D. (2016). Big Data's Disparate Impact. California Law Review, 104(3), 671-732.

BERENSON, H., BERNSTEIN, P. A., & STRONG, H. (1976). Consistency Conditions for Distributed Database Systems. ACM Transactions on Database Systems, 2(1), 98-102.

BRAZIL. (2020). General Law for the Protection of Personal Data (LGPD). Available at: https://www.gov.br/lgpd

BREWER, E., & KUBIATOWICZ, J. (2000). Preserving Data Integrity in Cloud-based Systems. ACM Computing Surveys, 52(1), 1-36.

BROOKS, D., & KOBAYASHI, H. (2021). In-Memory Computing: A New Paradigm for Big Data Processing. IEEE Transactions on Computers, 70(9), 1564-1575.

BROWN, M. (2020). Version Control Systems for Data: Managing Complex Machine Learning Workflows. O'Reilly Media.

BRYNJOLFSSON, E., & MCAFEE, A. (2014). The Second Machine Age: Work, Progress, and Prosperity in a Time of Brilliant Technologies. W. W. Norton & Company.

CODD, E. F. (1970). A Relational Model of Data for Large Shared Data Banks. Communications of the ACM, 13(6), 377-387.

CODD, E. F. (1970). A Relational Model of Data for Large Shared Data Banks. Communications of the ACM, 13(6), 377-387.

COX, P., & YU, T. (2015). Data Preservation in the Cloud: Techniques and Challenges. IEEE Cloud Computing, 2(1), 36-44.

DOSHI-VELEZ, F., & KIM, B. (2017). Towards a Rigorous Science of Interpretable Machine Learning. arXiv preprint arXiv:1702.08608.

EL MASRI, R., & NAVATHE, S. B. (2010). Fundamentals of Database Systems (6th Edition). Addison-Wesley.

EUROPEAN UNION. (2016). General Data Protection Regulation (GDPR). Available at: https://gdpr.eu/

GARTNER, I. (2021). Data Governance 2.0: Emerging Trends in Data Preservation. Gartner Research.

GONÇALVES, M. A. (2011). Data Mining: Concepts, Models, Methods, and Algorithms. Wiley-IEEE Press.

GOVERNMENT OF CANADA. (2000). Personal Information Protection and Electronic Documents Act (PIPEDA). Available at: https://www.priv.gc.ca/en/privacy-topics/privacy-laws-in-canada/the-personal-information-protection-and-electronic-documents-act-pipeda/

GOVERNMENT OF INDIA. (2019). Personal Data Protection Bill. Available at: https://www.meity.gov.in/content/personal-data-protection-bill-2019

HE, H., & GARCIA, E. A. (2009). Learning from Imbalanced Data. IEEE Transactions on Knowledge and Data Engineering, 21(9), 1263-1284.

HE, H., & GARCIA, E. A. (2009). Learning from Imbalanced Data. IEEE Transactions on Knowledge and Data Engineering, 21(9), 1263-1284.

HILDEBRANDT, M. (2015). Smart Technologies and the End(s) of Law: Novel Entanglements of Law and Technology. Edward Elgar Publishing.

INTERNATIONAL ORGANIZATION FOR STANDARDIZATION. (2012). ISO 14721: Space data and information transfer systems — Open archival information system (OAIS) — Reference model. ISO.

INTERNATIONAL ORGANIZATION FOR STANDARDIZATION. (2012). ISO 16363: Space data and information transfer systems — Audit and certification of trustworthy digital repositories. ISO.

INTERNATIONAL ORGANIZATION FOR STANDARDIZATION. (2015). ISO/IEC 27040: Information Technology — Security techniques — Storage security. ISO.

INTERNATIONAL ORGANIZATION FOR STANDARDIZATION. (2016). ISO 15489: Information and Documentation — Records Management. ISO.

INTERNATIONAL ORGANIZATION FOR STANDARDIZATION. (2022). ISO/IEC 27001: Information Security Management Systems — Requirements. ISO.

KANTARCI, B., ZEN, K. (2019). "Data Lineage for Machine Learning and AI: Techniques and Tools for Ensuring Data Integrity". Packt Publishing.

KITCHIN, R. (2014). The Data Revolution: Big Data, Open Data, Data Infrastructures and Their Consequences. SAGE Publications.

KORDIAK, T. (2019). Data Governance: A Practical Guide to Data Management and Governance in Your Organization. Packt Publishing.

LAMPORT, L. (1978). Time, Clocks, and the Ordering of Events in a Distributed System. Communications of the ACM, 21(7), 558-565.

MAYER-SCHÖNBERGER, V., & CUKIER, K. (2013). Big Data: A Revolution That Will Transform How We Live, Work, and Think. Eamon Dolan/Houghton Mifflin Harcourt.

MULLINS, C. S. (2012). Database Administration: The Complete Guide to DBA Practices and Procedures. Addison-Wesley.

OLIVIER, P., & CLARK, T. (2019). Data Governance: How to Design, Deploy, and Sustain an Effective Data Governance Program. Academic Press.

O'NEIL, C. (2016). Weapons of Math Destruction: How Big Data Increases Inequality and Threatens Democracy. Crown Publishing Group.

OPENAI. (2023). ChatGPT: Transformer-based Language Model. OpenAI Research Publication.

OPENAI. (2023). Ethical Considerations in AI: Addressing Bias in Historical Data. OpenAI Research Publication.

OTTO, B., & OSTERLE, H. (2015). Corporate Data Quality: Preconditions for Data Governance. Springer.

PARK, C., & SHIN, J. (2019). Cold Data Storage in the Era of Big Data: Trends and Future Directions. ACM Computing Surveys, 51(6), 1-28.

RAGHUNATHAN, S., & GROVER, V. (2002). Expurgation of Data: Legal, Ethical, and Operational Considerations. Journal of Information Systems, 16(4), 75-92.

RAMAKRISHNAN, R., & GEHRKE, J. (2000). Database Management Systems (3rd Edition). McGraw-Hill.

ROSENBERG, S., & KAUFMAN, M. (2018). Data Deletion: How to Identify and Delete Obsolete Data in Your Database. Database Trends and Applications.

RUSSELL, S., & NORVIG, P. (2010). Artificial Intelligence: A Modern Approach. Prentice Hall.

SHMOLIAN, G. (2017). Data Retention: Best Practices and Legal Requirements. Journal of Data Protection and Management, 4(2), 134-150.

SNODGRASS, R. T. (1987). The Temporal Query Language TQuel. ACM Transactions on Database Systems, 12(2), 247-298.

STALLINGS, W. (2013). Cryptography and Network Security: Principles and Practice. Pearson.

STATE OF CALIFORNIA. (2020). California Consumer Privacy Act (CCPA). Available at: https://oag.ca.gov/privacy/ccpa

STOICA, I., MORGAN, H., & ZAHARIA, M. (2020). A Survey of Modern Data Architectures. ACM Computing Surveys, 53(4), 1-36.

STONEBRAKER, M., & ÇETINTEMEL, U. (2005). "One Size Fits All": An Idea Whose Time Has Come and Gone. Proceedings of the 21st International Conference on Data Engineering, 2-11.

ZUBOFF, S. (2019). The Age of Surveillance Capitalism: The Fight for a Human Future at the New Frontier of Power. PublicAffairs.

16 Discover the Complete Collection "Artificial Intelligence and the Power of Data" – An Invitation to Transform Your Career and Knowledge.

The "Artificial Intelligence and the Power of Data" Collection was created for those who want not only to understand Artificial Intelligence (AI), but also to apply it strategically and practically.

In a series of carefully crafted volumes, I unravel complex concepts in a clear and accessible manner, ensuring the reader has a thorough understanding of AI and its impact on modern societies.

No matter what your level of familiarity with the topic, this collection turns the difficult into the didactic, theoretical into the applicable, and the technical into something powerful for your career.

16.1   Why buy this collection?

We are living through an unprecedented technological revolution, where AI is the driving force in areas such as medicine, finance, education, government, and entertainment.

The collection "Artificial Intelligence and the Power of Data" dives deep into all these sectors, with practical examples and reflections that go far beyond traditional concepts.

You'll find both the technical expertise and the ethical and social implications of AI encouraging you to see this technology not just as a tool, but as a true agent of transformation.

Each volume is a fundamental piece of this innovative puzzle: from machine learning to data governance and from ethics to practical application.

With the guidance of an experienced author who combines academic research with years of hands-on practice, this collection is more than a set of books – it's an indispensable guide for anyone looking to navigate and excel in this burgeoning field.

16.2   Target Audience of this Collection?

This collection is for everyone who wants to play a prominent role in the age of AI:

- ✓ Tech Professionals: Receive deep technical insights to expand their skills.

- ✓ Students and the Curious: have access to clear explanations that facilitate the understanding of the complex universe of AI.

- ✓ Managers, business leaders, and policymakers will also benefit from the strategic vision on AI, which is essential for making well-informed decisions.

- ✓ Professionals in Career Transition: Professionals in career transition or interested in specializing in AI will find here complete material to build their learning trajectory.

16.3   Much More Than Technique – A Complete Transformation.

This collection is not just a series of technical books; It is a tool for intellectual and professional growth.

With it, you go far beyond theory: each volume invites you to a deep reflection on the future of humanity in a world where machines and algorithms are increasingly present.

This is your invitation to master the knowledge that will define the future and become part of the transformation that Artificial Intelligence brings to the world.

Be a leader in your industry, master the skills the market demands, and prepare for the future with the "Artificial Intelligence and the Power of Data" collection.

This is not just a purchase; It is a decisive investment in your learning and professional development journey.

Prof. Marcão - Marcus Vinícius Pinto

M.Sc. in Information Technology.

Specialist in Artificial Intelligence, Data Governance and Information Architecture.

17 The Books of the Collection.

17.1 Data, Information and Knowledge in the era of Artificial Intelligence.

This book essentially explores the theoretical and practical foundations of Artificial Intelligence, from data collection to its transformation into intelligence. It focuses primarily on machine learning, AI training, and neural networks.

17.2 From Data to Gold: How to Turn Information into Wisdom in the Age of AI.

This book offers critical analysis on the evolution of Artificial Intelligence, from raw data to the creation of artificial wisdom, integrating neural networks, deep learning, and knowledge modeling.

It presents practical examples in health, finance, and education, and addresses ethical and technical challenges.

17.3 Challenges and Limitations of Data in AI.

The book offers an in-depth analysis of the role of data in the development of AI exploring topics such as quality, bias, privacy, security, and scalability with practical case studies in healthcare, finance, and public safety.

17.4 Historical Data in Databases for AI: Structures, Preservation, and Purge.

This book investigates how historical data management is essential to the success of AI projects. It addresses the relevance of ISO standards to ensure quality and safety, in addition to analyzing trends and innovations in data processing.

17.5   Controlled Vocabulary for Data Dictionary: A Complete Guide.

This comprehensive guide explores the advantages and challenges of implementing controlled vocabularies in the context of AI and information science. With a detailed approach, it covers everything from the naming of data elements to the interactions between semantics and cognition.

17.6   Data Curation and Management for the Age of AI.

This book presents advanced strategies for transforming raw data into valuable insights, with a focus on meticulous curation and efficient data management. In addition to technical solutions, it addresses ethical and legal issues, empowering the reader to face the complex challenges of information.

17.7   Information Architecture.

The book addresses data management in the digital age, combining theory and practice to create efficient and scalable AI systems, with insights into modeling and ethical and legal challenges.

17.8   Fundamentals: The Essentials of Mastering Artificial Intelligence.

An essential work for anyone who wants to master the key concepts of AI, with an accessible approach and practical examples. The book explores innovations such as Machine Learning and Natural Language Processing, as well as ethical and legal challenges, and offers a clear view of the impact of AI on various industries.

17.9   LLMS - Large-Scale Language Models.

This essential guide helps you understand the revolution of Large-Scale Language Models (LLMs) in AI.

The book explores the evolution of GPTs and the latest innovations in human-computer interaction, offering practical insights into their impact on industries such as healthcare, education, and finance.

17.10   Machine Learning: Fundamentals and Advances.

This book offers a comprehensive overview of supervised and unsupervised algorithms, deep neural networks, and federated learning. In addition to addressing issues of ethics and explainability of models.

17.11   Inside Synthetic Minds.

This book reveals how these 'synthetic minds' are redefining creativity, work, and human interactions. This work presents a detailed analysis of the challenges and opportunities provided by these technologies, exploring their profound impact on society.

17.12   The Issue of Copyright.

This book invites the reader to explore the future of creativity in a world where human-machine collaboration is a reality, addressing questions about authorship, originality, and intellectual property in the age of generative AIs.

17.13   1121 Questions and Answers: From Basic to Complex – Part 1 to 4.

Organized into four volumes, these questions serve as essential practical guides to mastering key AI concepts.

Part 1 addresses information, data, geoprocessing, the evolution of artificial intelligence, its historical milestones and basic concepts.

Part 2 delves into complex concepts such as machine learning, natural language processing, computer vision, robotics, and decision algorithms.

Part 3 addresses issues such as data privacy, work automation, and the impact of large-scale language models (LLMs).

Part 4 explores the central role of data in the age of artificial intelligence, delving into the fundamentals of AI and its applications in areas such as mental health, government, and anti-corruption.

17.14   The Definitive Glossary of Artificial Intelligence.

This glossary presents more than a thousand artificial intelligence concepts clearly explained, covering topics such as Machine Learning, Natural Language Processing, Computer Vision, and AI Ethics.

- Part 1 contemplates concepts starting with the letters A to D.
- Part 2 contemplates concepts initiated by the letters E to M.
- Part 3 contemplates concepts starting with the letters N to Z.

17.15 Prompt Engineering - Volumes 1 to 6.

This collection covers all the fundamentals of prompt engineering, providing a complete foundation for professional development.

With a rich variety of prompts for areas such as leadership, digital marketing, and information technology, it offers practical examples to improve clarity, decision-making, and gain valuable insights.

The volumes cover the following subjects:

- Volume 1: Fundamentals. Structuring Concepts and History of Prompt Engineering.
- Volume 2: Tools and Technologies, State and Context Management, and Ethics and Security.
- Volume 3: Language Models, Tokenization, and Training Methods.
- Volume 4: How to Ask Right Questions.
- Volume 5: Case Studies and Errors.
- Volume 6: The Best Prompts.

17.16 Guide to Being a Prompt Engineer – Volumes 1 and 2.

The collection explores the advanced fundamentals and skills required to be a successful prompt engineer, highlighting the benefits, risks, and the critical role this role plays in the development of artificial intelligence.

Volume 1 covers crafting effective prompts, while Volume 2 is a guide to understanding and applying the fundamentals of Prompt Engineering.

17.17   Data Governance with AI – Volumes 1 to 3.

Find out how to implement effective data governance with this comprehensive collection. Offering practical guidance, this collection covers everything from data architecture and organization to protection and quality assurance, providing a complete view to transform data into strategic assets.

Volume 1 addresses practices and regulations. Volume 2 explores in depth the processes, techniques, and best practices for conducting effective audits on data models. Volume 3 is your definitive guide to deploying data governance with AI.

17.18   Algorithm Governance.

This book looks at the impact of algorithms on society, exploring their foundations and addressing ethical and regulatory issues.

It addresses transparency, accountability, and bias, with practical solutions for auditing and monitoring algorithms in sectors such as finance, health, and education.

17.19   From IT Professional to AI Expert: The Ultimate Guide to a Successful Career Transition.

For Information Technology professionals, the transition to AI represents a unique opportunity to enhance skills and contribute to the development of innovative solutions that shape the future.

In this book, we investigate the reasons for making this transition, the essential skills, the best learning path, and the prospects for the future of the IT job market.

17.20   Intelligent Leadership with AI: Transform Your Team and Drive Results.

This book reveals how artificial intelligence can revolutionize team management and maximize organizational performance.

By combining traditional leadership techniques with AI-powered insights, such as predictive analytics-based leadership, you'll learn how to optimize processes, make more strategic decisions, and create more efficient and engaged teams.

17.21   Impacts and Transformations: Complete Collection.

This collection offers a comprehensive and multifaceted analysis of the transformations brought about by Artificial Intelligence in contemporary society.

- Volume 1: Challenges and Solutions in the Detection of Texts Generated by Artificial Intelligence.
- Volume 2: The Age of Filter Bubbles. Artificial Intelligence and the Illusion of Freedom.
- Volume 3: Content Creation with AI - How to Do It?
- Volume 4: The Singularity Is Closer Than You Think.
- Volume 5: Human Stupidity versus Artificial Intelligence.
- Volume 6: The Age of Stupidity! A Cult of Stupidity?
- Volume 7: Autonomy in Motion: The Intelligent Vehicle Revolution.
- Volume 8: Poiesis and Creativity with AI.

- Volume 9: Perfect Duo: AI + Automation.
- Volume 10: Who Holds the Power of Data?

17.22   Big Data with AI: Complete Collection.

The collection covers everything from the technological fundamentals and architecture of Big Data to the administration and glossary of essential technical terms.

The collection also discusses the future of humanity's relationship with the enormous volume of data generated in the databases of training in Big Data structuring.

- Volume 1: Fundamentals.
- Volume 2: Architecture.
- Volume 3: Implementation.
- Volume 4: Administration.
- Volume 5: Essential Themes and Definitions.
- Volume 6: Data Warehouse, Big Data, and AI.

18 About the author.

I'm Marcus Pinto, better known as Prof. Marcão, a specialist in information technology, information architecture and artificial intelligence.

With more than four decades of dedicated work and research, I have built a solid and recognized trajectory, always focused on making technical knowledge accessible and applicable to all those who seek to understand and stand out in this transformative field.

My experience spans strategic consulting, education and authorship, as well as an extensive performance as an information architecture analyst.

This experience enables me to offer innovative solutions adapted to the constantly evolving needs of the technological market, anticipating trends and creating bridges between technical knowledge and practical impact.

Over the years, I have developed comprehensive and in-depth expertise in data, artificial intelligence, and information governance – areas that have become essential for building robust and secure systems capable of handling the vast volume of data that shapes today's world.

My book collection, available on Amazon, reflects this expertise, addressing topics such as Data Governance, Big Data, and Artificial Intelligence with a clear focus on practical applications and strategic vision.

Author of more than 150 books, I investigate the impact of artificial intelligence in multiple spheres, exploring everything from its technical bases to the ethical issues that become increasingly urgent with the adoption of this technology on a large scale.

In my lectures and mentorships, I share not only the value of AI, but also the challenges and responsibilities that come with its implementation – elements that I consider essential for ethical and conscious adoption.

I believe that technological evolution is an inevitable path. My books are a proposed guide on this path, offering deep and accessible insights for those who want not only to understand, but to master the technologies of the future.

With a focus on education and human development, I invite you to join me on this transformative journey, exploring the possibilities and challenges that this digital age has in store for us.

19 How to contact prof. Marcão.

19.1 For lectures, training and business mentoring.

marcao.tecno@gmail.com

19.2 Prof. Marcão, on Linkedin.

https://bit.ly/linkedin_profmarcao

www.ingramcontent.com/pod-product-compliance
Lightning Source LLC
LaVergne TN
LVHW051700050326
832903LV00032B/3928